Travel Gu

MW01490973

Welcome to our Travel Gu.... .. j..u..i, y..u. .....spensaole companion for exploring this captivating country. Whether you're a history buff, a foodie, an adventurer, or someone simply looking to unwind, this comprehensive guide has got you covered.

Are you curious about the ancient ruins of Petra, the rose-red city that has captivated travelers for centuries? Or perhaps you're eager to float in the mineral-rich waters of the Dead Sea? Maybe you're a gastronome looking to delve into Jordan's rich culinary landscape? From the bustling streets of Amman to the tranquil deserts of Wadi Rum, this guide offers detailed insights into Jordan's diverse attractions, culture, and history.

Our guide is meticulously organized to serve as both a planning tool and an on-the-ground resource. It begins with essential background information, including a history of Jordan, key cities, and the country's geography and climate. We also provide practical advice on getting to Jordan, visa requirements, and transportation options within the country.

Accommodation is a crucial aspect of any trip, and our guide offers a curated list of the best places to stay, from luxury resorts to budget-friendly hotels. Foodies will appreciate our in-depth look at Jordan's food culture, including the best restaurants, coffee shops, and markets across various cities.

For the explorers, we've included a comprehensive list of top attractions in key regions, along with day trips and excursions to make the most of your visit. And because we understand that travel is more than just sightseeing, we've also included sections on art galleries, museums, and even the nightlife in Jordan.

With maps, FAQs, and practical tips, this guide is designed to make your journey as smooth as possible. Whether you're a first-time visitor or a seasoned traveler, "The Ultimate Guide to Jordan" is your go-to resource for a trip of a lifetime.

Table of Contents

5

1   Introduction

Discover the Magic of Jordan: An Unforgettable Journey Awaits

Welcome to Jordan, a land of mesmerizing beauty and contrasts, from the Jordan River to the arid desert of Wadi Rum. This Middle Eastern gem is a haven for adventure seekers, history buffs, and those seeking to understand the rich tapestry of cultures that have shaped this region for millennia.

A Land Steeped in History

Jordan's history is as vast as the desert sands that sweep across its southern regions. Home to some of the world's oldest civilizations, Jordan has been inhabited by humans since the Paleolithic period. Over the centuries, it has seen the rise and fall of numerous empires, from the ancient Nabateans and Romans to the Islamic Caliphates and Ottoman Empire.

The echoes of these civilizations are etched into the country's landscape, from the majestic ruins of Petra, a UNESCO World Heritage Site often described as the eighth wonder of the world, to the Roman amphitheater in the heart of Amman. In Jordan, history is not confined to textbooks but is a living, breathing entity that you can explore and experience firsthand.

Natural Wonders Abound

But Jordan's appeal extends beyond its historical sites. The country is blessed with natural wonders that are as diverse as they are stunning. The Dead Sea, the lowest point on earth, is a must-visit for its therapeutic mud and buoyant waters. The Wadi

Rum, also known as the Valley of the Moon, offers breathtaking desert landscapes that have served as the backdrop for numerous films.

For those who prefer verdant landscapes, the Dana Biosphere Reserve, Jordan's largest nature reserve, provides a refreshing contrast with its diverse flora and fauna. And let's not forget the Red Sea resort of Aqaba, a paradise for snorkelers and divers with its vibrant coral reefs and crystal-clear waters.

A Taste of Jordanian Hospitality
Jordan is not just about historical monuments and natural beauty. It's about the spirit of the people who call this land home. Known for their warm hospitality, Jordanians are eager to share their culture, traditions, and, of course, their food. Jordanian cuisine is a gastronomic delight, with dishes like mansaf, falafel, and kunafa taking center stage.

A Safe Haven in the Middle East
Despite being in a region often associated with turmoil, Jordan stands out as a safe and stable destination. The country is a testament to peaceful coexistence, with its diverse religious and ethnic communities living together in harmony. Whether you're wandering through the bustling souks of Amman or exploring the remote desert landscapes, you'll feel welcomed and secure.

The Journey of a Lifetime
Jordan is more than just a travel destination. It's a journey into a vibrant and enduring civilization that has left its mark on both history and humanity. It's a place where the past and present coexist, where age-old traditions blend seamlessly with modernity.

Whether you're standing at the top of Mount Nebo, looking out onto the Promised Land as Moses once did, floating in the Dead Sea, or gazing at the stars in the desert of Wadi Rum, you'll find that Jordan has a way of touching your soul and capturing your heart.

So come, immerse yourself in the magic of Jordan. Experience its rich history, stunning landscapes, delectable cuisine, and warm hospitality. A world of adventure, discovery, and unforgettable experiences awaits you in this captivating corner of the Middle East. Your journey of a lifetime begins here. Welcome to Jordan.

1.1   Map of Jordan

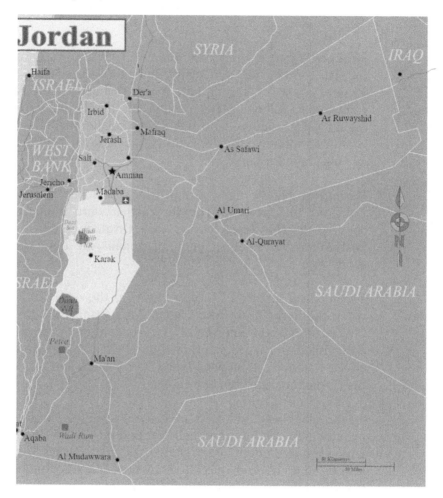

1.2   A History of Jordan

Jordan, officially known as the Hashemite Kingdom of Jordan, is a country with a rich history that dates back to the Paleolithic period. The region has seen the rise and fall of numerous civilizations, each leaving its mark and contributing to the country's cultural heritage.

The earliest evidence of human habitation in Jordan dates back to the Lower Paleolithic period, around 250,000 years ago. The region was later inhabited by the Canaanites and the Ammonites, who established the Ammonite Kingdom around the 13th century BC. The Nabateans, famous for their capital city of Petra, also thrived in the region from the 4th century BC to the 2nd century AD.

Jordan was part of the Roman Empire from the 1st century BC to the 4th century AD, and many Roman ruins, such as those in Jerash, attest to the grandeur of Roman architecture and civilization. Following the decline of the Roman Empire, the region was conquered by the Byzantine Empire and later the Islamic Caliphate in the 7th century, marking the beginning of the Islamic era in Jordan.

During the Middle Ages, Jordan was a strategic location in the Crusades, and several Crusader castles were built across the country. In the 16th century, the Ottoman Empire annexed Jordan, and it remained under Ottoman rule until the end of World War I.

The modern history of Jordan began in the early 20th century when the Great Arab Revolt against the Ottoman Empire led to the creation of the Emirate of Transjordan under the Hashemite Emir Abdullah I, a protectorate of the British Empire. In 1946, the emirate gained full independence from Britain and was renamed the Hashemite Kingdom of Jordan.

Jordan has been involved in several conflicts in the region, including the 1948 Arab-Israeli War and the Six-Day War in 1967, which resulted in the loss of the West Bank to Israel. The country also faced a civil war in 1970, known as Black September, when the Jordanian army clashed with Palestinian guerrillas.

In recent years, Jordan has been relatively stable compared to its neighbors. The country has absorbed a significant number of refugees from conflicts in neighboring countries, particularly Iraq and Syria, which has put a strain on its resources. Despite these challenges, Jordan continues to play a significant role in regional diplomacy and maintains peaceful relations with many countries.

As of 2023, Jordan is a constitutional monarchy under the reign of King Abdullah II. The country faces several challenges, including economic issues, water scarcity, and the ongoing refugee crisis. However, it remains a key player in the Middle East, maintaining its commitment to peace and stability in the region.

Please note that this is a brief summary and does not cover all aspects of Jordan's extensive history. For a more detailed account, I recommend further reading or consulting a history expert.

1.3   Cities in Jordan

Amman

Amman, the capital city of Jordan, is a bustling metropolis with a mix of modernity and tradition. It is one of the oldest continuously inhabited cities in the world, with a history dating back to the Neolithic period. The city is known for its ancient ruins, including the Amman Citadel and the Roman Theater. It also boasts a vibrant arts scene, bustling markets, and a variety of restaurants serving delicious local and international cuisine.

Jerash

Jerash is a city in Jordan known for the ruins of the ancient Greco-Roman city of Gerasa, also referred to as Antioch on the Golden River. It is considered one of the most important and best preserved Roman cities in the Near East. The city is home to the ancient Hadrian's Arch, the Corinthian columns of the Temple of Artemis, and the large and impressive Jerash theatre.

Dead Sea

The Dead Sea, bordered by Jordan to the east and Israel and Palestine to the west, is one of the world's saltiest bodies of water. It is also the lowest point on the surface of the Earth. The high salt concentration allows swimmers to easily float on the surface. The mineral-rich mud is also used for therapeutic and cosmetic treatments.

Petra

Petra, also known as the Rose City due to the color of the stone from which it is carved, is one of the most famous archaeological sites in the world. It was the capital of the Nabatean Kingdom and is known for its intricate rock-cut architecture, including the iconic Treasury (Al-Khazneh). Petra is a UNESCO World Heritage Site and one of the New Seven Wonders of the World.

Wadi Rum

Wadi Rum, also known as the Valley of the Moon, is a valley cut into the sandstone and granite rock in southern Jordan. It is known for its stunning desert landscapes, prehistoric rock carvings, and natural arches. It's a popular destination for hiking, rock climbing, camel and horse safaris, and overnight camping in Bedouin tents.

Aqaba

Aqaba is the only coastal city in Jordan, located at the northeastern tip of the Red Sea. It is a popular spot for water sports like snorkeling and scuba diving, with stunning coral reefs and marine life. The city also has a rich history, with sites like the medieval Aqaba Fortress and the archaeological site of Ayla.

1.4   The Population of Jordan

Jordan: A Melting Pot of Cultures

Jordan, a country known for its rich history and warm hospitality, is also home to a diverse population. The country's population is estimated to be around 10.6 million people, with the capital city, Amman, being the most populous, housing around 1.27 million residents. Other major cities include Zarqa with a population of approximately 792,665 and Irbid with around 569,068 inhabitants.

Ethnic Diversity

The ethnic composition of Jordan is predominantly Arab, accounting for around 94% of the population. However, the country is also home to a variety of ethnic minorities that add to its cultural richness. These include Circassians, Chechens, Armenians, and Kurds, each contributing their unique traditions and customs to the Jordanian cultural tapestry.

Circassians and Chechens

Circassians and Chechens, originating from the North Caucasus region, have been a part of Jordanian society for over a century. They have integrated well into the Jordanian society while preserving their unique culture and traditions.

Armenians

The Armenian community in Jordan, although small, has a significant presence. They are mainly concentrated in the capital, Amman, and have contributed significantly to the arts and business sectors in Jordan.

Kurds

The Kurdish community in Jordan is also small but has a distinct cultural presence. They maintain their unique language and cultural practices, adding to the multicultural fabric of Jordan.

Palestinians, Syrians, and Egyptians

In addition to these ethnic minorities, Jordan has also been a refuge for many people in the region. Palestinians constitute a significant portion of the population due to the ongoing Israeli-Palestinian conflict. More recently, the Syrian civil war has led to an influx of Syrian refugees, who now constitute around 13.3% of the population. There is also a significant Egyptian community in Jordan, making up around 6.7% of the population.

Cultural Harmony

Despite the diversity, Jordan has managed to maintain a harmonious society where different cultures coexist peacefully. The Jordanian government has played a significant role in ensuring the integration of these diverse communities into the broader Jordanian society.

Jordan's population is a vibrant mix of different ethnicities and cultures. This diversity is a testament to the country's rich history as a crossroads of civilizations and its ongoing role as a haven for those seeking refuge. The multicultural fabric of Jordanian society is one of its greatest strengths, making it a fascinating destination for travelers seeking to experience a rich blend of cultures in a single nation.

1.5 Languages of Jordan and common phrases

Here's an overview of the languages spoken in Jordan:
Arabic is the official language of Jordan and is spoken by almost the entire population, including minority communities. The form of Arabic used in Jordan is known as Jordanian Arabic, a dialect continuum of mutually intelligible varieties of Arabic spoken by the population of the Hashemite Kingdom of Jordan.

Although Arabic is the primary language, **English** is also widely spoken, especially in the cities. Many Jordanians have traveled or studied abroad, making English a commonly understood language, particularly among the younger generation and in business and tourism sectors.

As a tourist, it's always helpful to learn a few local phrases. Here are some basic Arabic phrases that might come in handy:
1. **Hello**: Marhaba

2. **Thank you**: Shukran
3. **Yes**: Na'am
4. **No**: La
5. **Please**: Min fadlak (to a man) / Min fadlik (to a woman)
6. **Excuse me**: Afwan
7. **Do you speak English?**: Hal tatakallam al-ingliziya?

Remember, a little effort goes a long way and locals appreciate it when tourists make an effort to speak their language. Happy traveling!

1.6 The Culture and Religions of Jordan

Culture and Religions of Jordan

Jordan is a country rich in history, culture, and religious diversity. It is a tolerant, Islamic state that welcomes all religions. The culture of Jordan is deeply rooted in its Islamic heritage and Arab traditions, making it a vibrant and fascinating destination for tourists.

Religion in Jordan

Religion plays a significant role in the lives of Jordanians. The state religion is Sunni Islam, and about 92% of Jordanians are followers. There is also a small percentage of Shia and Sufi Muslims in the country. However, Jordan is known for its religious tolerance, and it welcomes all religions. About 8% of the population are Christians, belonging to various denominations such as the Greek Orthodox Church, Greek Catholics, Roman Catholics, Syrian Orthodox, and Coptic Orthodox.

Language and Common Phrases

The official language of Jordan is Arabic. However, English is widely spoken among the middle and upper classes and is commonly used in commerce and government. Among the younger generation, English is often the second language of choice.

For tourists, knowing a few common Arabic phrases can enhance their travel experience. Here are a few:

1. *Marhaba* - Hello
2. *Shukran* - Thank you
3. *Afwan* - You're welcome
4. *Min fadlak* (to a male) / *Min fadlik* (to a female) - Please

5. *Naam* - Yes
6. *La* - No
7. *Ma'assalama* – Goodbye

Cultural Diversity

Jordan is a country of cultural diversity. Its population is a mix of people who have inhabited the region for thousands of years, including Circassians, Armenians, and Palestinians. This diversity is reflected in the country's traditions, cuisine, music, and festivals.

Jordanians are known for their hospitality and respect for others. It is common for locals to invite tourists into their homes for a meal. This hospitality is a key part of Jordanian culture and is deeply rooted in Bedouin traditions.

1.7   Currency in Jordan

Currency in Jordan

The official currency of Jordan is the Jordanian dinar, abbreviated as JOD. The dinar is further divided into 100 qirsh (also called piastres) or 1000 fulus. The Jordanian dinar has been the currency of Jordan since 1950.

Exchange Rate

The exchange rate of the Jordanian dinar is pegged to the United States Dollar at 0.709 JOD = 1 USD. This means that the value of the dinar is directly linked to the value of the US dollar.

Best Methods to Pay in Jordan

In Jordan, cash is widely accepted and often preferred, especially for small purchases in local markets or taxis. Credit and debit cards are also widely accepted in hotels, restaurants, and larger shops. ATMs are readily available in cities and larger towns, where you can withdraw cash in Jordanian dinars.

Currency Exchange

Currency can be exchanged at banks, exchange bureaus, and some hotels. It's advisable to compare rates before exchanging your money as they can vary. Also, keep in mind that some smaller establishments and street vendors might not accept large denomination notes, so it's useful to have a variety of smaller notes and coins on hand.

Withdraw Cash

ATMs are a convenient way to access your money while traveling in Jordan. They can be found in most cities and larger towns. Be aware that your bank may charge you a fee for overseas withdrawals. It's also a good idea to inform your bank of your travel plans to avoid any potential blocks on your card.

Remember, it's always a good idea to have a mix of payment options when you travel. A combination of local currency, a credit or debit card, and perhaps a small amount of US dollars as a backup, can be a good strategy.

1.8   Geography and Climate of Jordan

Geography of Jordan

Jordan is situated geographically in Southwest Asia, south of Syria, west of Iraq, northwest of Saudi Arabia, and east of Israel. The country's terrain varies significantly across its regions. On the eastern desert plateau, the average elevation is 3,000 feet. In contrast, the western mountains rise to 5,700 feet. The lowest point in the country, and indeed the lowest land point on earth, is the Dead Sea, which is over 1,300 feet below sea level.

Climate of Jordan

Jordan's climate varies from Mediterranean in the west to desert in the east and south, but the land is generally arid. The proximity of the Mediterranean Sea has a significant influence on the climate, especially in the western part of the country. The climate is generally of the Mediterranean type, but that applies mainly to the higher lands. Further east, towards the desert, it is hotter during the day and can get quite cold at night.

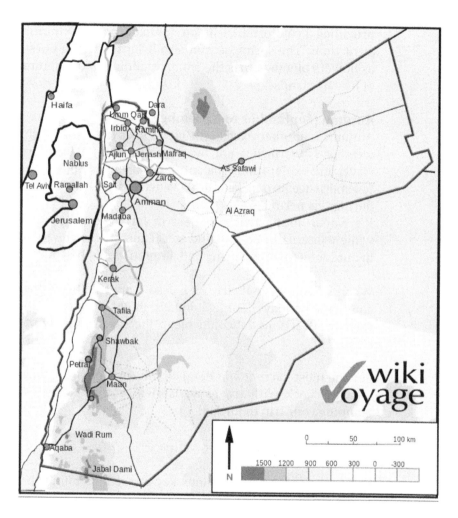

1.9   Best time to visit Jordan

Best Times to Visit Jordan
Jordan is a country with a diverse climate, and the best time to visit can depend on your interests and the activities you plan to

21

do. However, there are generally two periods that are considered the most favorable for visiting Jordan.

Spring (March to May)
Spring is a popular time to visit Jordan. The weather during this period is more temperate, making it ideal for outdoor activities and sightseeing. The temperatures range between 61°F and 99°F, providing a comfortable climate for exploring the country's many attractions. The spring season also brings with it a burst of color as flowers bloom across the country, adding to the natural beauty of Jordan's landscapes.

Autumn (September to November)
Autumn is another excellent time to visit Jordan. Like spring, the weather is warm but not overly hot, making it comfortable for travel and exploration. The autumn season also offers the chance to experience Jordan's cultural events and festivals that take place during this period.
It's worth noting that summers in Jordan can be hot and dry, while winters can be cold and wet. Therefore, if you're interested in outdoor activities, spring and autumn would be your best bet.

When planning your trip, it's also important to consider the country's holidays. Some holidays might result in closures of certain attractions or could mean increased crowds at popular sites.

For the most current and detailed information, it's always a good idea to check with travel advisories or tour operators before planning your trip to Jordan.

1.10 Key attractions in Jordan

Below are some of the various key attractions found throughout Jordan.

Petra
Known as the Rose City due to the color of the stone from which it is carved, Petra is an archaeological city that dates back to 300 B.C. It is Jordan's most-visited tourist attraction and a UNESCO World Heritage site. The city is famous for its rock-cut architecture and water conduit system.

Dead Sea

The Dead Sea is one of the world's saltiest bodies of water, and it's also the lowest point on the surface of the earth. Its high salt concentration allows you to float on the water easily. The mud from the sea is also known for its therapeutic properties.

Wadi Rum

Also known as The Valley of the Moon, Wadi Rum is a desert valley cut into the sandstone and granite rock. It's a popular destination for climbing, hiking, and camel and horse safaris. The area has been inhabited by many human cultures since prehistoric times, with many cultures leaving their mark in the form of rock paintings, graffiti, and temples.

Jerash Ruins

Jerash is home to the ruins of the ancient city of Gerasa, also referred to as Antioch on the Golden River. It's one of the most important and best preserved Roman cities in the Near East. It was a city of the Decapolis and is now a popular tourist attraction.

Aqaba
Aqaba is a Jordanian coastal city situated at the northeastern tip of the Red Sea. It's the largest city on the Gulf of Aqaba and Jordan's only coastal city. The city is best known today as a diving and beach resort and is home to upscale hotels and shopping centers.

Amman
Amman, the capital of Jordan, is a modern city with numerous ancient ruins. Atop Jabal al-Qala'a hill, the historic Citadel includes the pillars of the Roman Temple of Hercules and the 8th-century Umayyad Palace complex, known for its grand dome.

Dana Biosphere Reserve

Dana Biosphere Reserve is Jordan's largest nature reserve, located in south-central Jordan. It's a world of natural treasures, including hiking trails, eco-tourism facilities, and a wide variety of flora and fauna.

Umm Qais

Umm Qais, a town in northern Jordan, is famous for its beautiful Ottoman village, its views over the Sea of Galilee, and the ruins of the ancient Gadara.

1.11 Interesting facts about Jordan

Here are some interesting and lesser-known facts about Jordan.

Home to Numerous Archaeological Sites

Jordan is a treasure trove of history, with over 100,000 archaeological sites. Only 15% of the famous city of Petra has been explored, leaving much of its history still buried beneath the sands.

Oldest Dam in the World

The Jawa Dam in Jordan dates back to the 4th millennium BC, making it the oldest dam in the world. This is a testament to the advanced engineering skills of the ancient civilizations that inhabited the region.

Lowest Point on Earth

The Dead Sea, located in Jordan, is the lowest point on Earth. This unique body of water is famous for its high salt concentration, which allows people to float effortlessly on the surface.

Rich in Natural and Cultural Attractions

From the red desert landscapes of Wadi Rum to the ancient Roman ruins of Jerash, Jordan is home to a wealth of natural and cultural attractions. It's a country that offers something for every type of traveler.

A Kingdom in Western Asia

Jordan is an Arab kingdom located in Western Asia, on the East Bank of the Jordan River. Despite its small size, it's a country rich in history, culture, and natural beauty.

Famous Visitors

Jordan has attracted many famous visitors over the years, including numerous Hollywood stars who have come to film in its unique locations. The country's landscapes have served as the backdrop for several blockbuster movies.

Remember, these are just a few highlights. Jordan is a country that's full of surprises and there's always more to discover!

1.12 Ten Prominent People that Hail from Jordan

Below are the names of some of the most famous people from Jordan.

- ○ **King Abdullah II**
  The current King of Jordan, Abdullah II has been reigning since 1999. He is known for his efforts in modernizing Jordan and his advocacy for peace in the Middle East.

- ○ **Queen Rania**
  The wife of King Abdullah II, Queen Rania is known for her advocacy for education, health, community empowerment, youth, cross-cultural dialogue, and micro-finance. She is also a global figure with a significant online presence.

- ○ **Prince Ghazi bin Muhammad**
  A Jordanian prince, professor of philosophy, and claims to be a direct descendant of the Islamic prophet Muhammad.

- ○ **Hussein Bin Ali Sharif Of Mecca**
  A Hashemite sharif of Mecca and King of Hejaz, who played a significant role in the Arab Revolt against the Ottoman Empire during World War I.

28

- **Sirhan Sirhan**
  A Palestinian with Jordanian citizenship, Sirhan Sirhan is known for the assassination of U.S. Senator Robert F. Kennedy.

- **Khaled Mashal**
  A Palestinian political leader and the leader of the Islamic Palestinian organization Hamas.

- **Nadim Sawalha**
  A Jordanian-British actor, known for his roles in various British TV dramas and films.

- **Ayah Marar**
  A Jordanian singer, songwriter, performer, radio show host and label owner based in the UK.

- **King Deco**
  A Jordanian singer and songwriter who has made a name for herself in the world of indie pop.

- **Hala Abusham**
  A popular Jordanian social media influencer.

1.13 FAQ's when travelling to Jordan

These frequently asked questions and their answers may help the first-time visitor to Jordan.

What should I wear in Jordan?
Modest, conservative clothing is recommended when visiting historical and religious sites in Jordan. Both men and women should cover knees and shoulders. Wearing shorts or sleeveless tops may not be allowed at some sites. Outside of historic sites, casual lightweight clothing along with a light sweater or jacket for the evenings is recommended.

What is the official language of Jordan?

The official language of Jordan is Arabic. However, English is widely spoken especially in the cities and by the younger generation.

What currency is used in Jordan?
The official currency of Jordan is the Jordanian Dinar (JOD).

Do I need a visa to visit Jordan?
Most nationalities can obtain a visa upon arrival at the airport and land borders. However, check visa requirements for your nationality before traveling. Single-entry tourist visas are normally valid for 30 days. Multiple entry visas are available.

Is it safe to travel to Jordan?
Yes, Jordan is generally considered safe for travel. However, like any other destination, it's always important to stay aware of your surroundings and follow local advice.

What is the best time to visit Jordan?
The best time to visit Jordan is in the spring (March-May) and fall (September-November). The weather is warm and sunny, but not too hot. Spring has the advantage of seeing Jordan's beautiful wildflowers bloom.

What languages are spoken in Jordan?
The official language is Arabic. Many Jordanians in the cities and in the tourist industry will speak English. Learning a few basic Arabic greetings and phrases can help when interacting with locals.

What are the top attractions and activities for visitors to Jordan?
Top attractions include Petra, the ancient Nabatean city carved in stone; the desert of Wadi Rum with amazing landscapes; the Dead Sea; Jerash, a Roman provincial city with restored ruins; Amman, the modern capital with ancient sites; Aqaba, coastal city with Red Sea beaches and coral reefs. Activities include hiking, trekking, camping, snorkeling, SCUBA diving, etc.

What is Jordanian food like? What should I try?
Jordanian cuisine features lamb, yogurt, veggies like eggplant, hummus and falafel made from chickpeas, fresh salads, rice, and

flatbreads. Dishes to try include mansaf (lamb in yogurt sauce), mujaddara (rice & lentils), kebabs, and knafeh for dessert. Jordanian feasts with meze (small plates) are very common.

Is it easy for tourists to get around Jordan?
Yes, Jordan has good infrastructure making travel relatively easy. There are buses and shared taxis between cities, and plenty of taxis in cities. Many choose to hire a car and driver for greater flexibility. Tour packages can also arrange transportation as desired.

Can I drink tap water in Jordan?
It's generally recommended to drink bottled water in Jordan.

Is it customary to tip in Jordan?
Yes, tipping is customary in Jordan. A 10% tip is generally expected in restaurants and for services.

What should I know about visiting Petra?
- Purchase a ticket in advance and arrive early (before 8 am) to beat the crowds.
- Wear good walking shoes as it requires a lot of walking on uneven terrain.
- Be prepared to pay for rides on horses or camels within the site if you don't want to walk.
- One day is enough time to see the highlights, but 2-3 days allows you to explore more fully.
- Stay overnight in nearby Wadi Musa town to be close to Petra.

What are some top destinations in Amman?
- The Citadel hill area with the Temple of Hercules and the Jordan Archaeological Museum
- Downtown Amman for street food, coffee shops, and the hubbub of city life
- The Roman Theatre and nearby souks (markets)
- The Royal Automobile Museum if you're a car enthusiast
- The Jordan Museum for an excellent overview of Jordanian history and culture

What should I know about visiting the Dead Sea?
- Stay at one of the resorts to access Dead Sea beaches and mineral-rich mud.

- Don't shave before swimming - the water will irritate cuts.
- Keep water away from eyes, nose, and mouth as it is very salty.
- Floating is easy due to the high salt content.
- Take a dip but don't stay in too long to avoid overly dry skin.
- Check spa services like Dead Sea mud wraps at your resort.

What is the best way to experience Wadi Rum?
- Staying overnight at one of the Bedouin camps allows you to see the spectacular sunrises/sunsets.
- Joining a 4x4 jeep tour is the most common way to explore the area.
- Hiking and rock climbing are also popular activities.
- Booking through local Bedouin operators helps support the communities.
- Avoid very hot summer months.

What options are there for getting to Jordan?
- Queen Alia International Airport in Amman is the main airport. It has connections from Europe, Asia, Africa, and the Middle East.
- Some fly into Aqaba Airport from Europe for access to Petra and Wadi Rum.
- Israel's airports can be used to cross at land borders like the Sheikh Hussein Crossing.
- Ferries run from Egypt to Aqaba. Buses run to Jordan from Syria, Israel, and Saudi Arabia.

What kind of electrical adapters do I need in Jordan?
- Jordan uses 220V electricity with Type C, D, F, G, J plugs.
- Type C plugs with two round prongs are the most common.
- Pack a universal adapter to be prepared for the different plug types.

How do I get around within cities in Jordan?
- Taxis are widely available, though metered fares are often not used. Agree on a price before getting in.
- Uber and Careem ride services are popular options.
- Buses connect major sites like the Citadel and Roman Theatre in Amman.
- Walking around downtowns and city centers is doable for shorter distances.

What kind of accommodations are available for travelers?

- Jordan has hotels ranging from budget hostels to luxury resorts.
- Furnished apartments are an option for long-term stays.
- Campsites and eco-lodges available near Petra, Wadi Rum, and nature reserves.
- Airbnb offers apartments, rooms, and houses for rent throughout Jordan.
- Bedouin campsites in Wadi Rum provide a unique desert experience.

Should I be concerned about safety as a solo female traveler?

- Jordan is generally safe, but women may get unwanted attention. Dressing conservatively can help avoid hassles.
- Use common sense, avoid isolated areas at night, and consider group tours for longer adventures.
- Taxi rides alone as a female traveler is fine during the daytime. Sit in the back seat.
- In museums and other tourist sites, you will see both local and foreign women traveling alone.

What is the best way to find tour guides?

- Ask your hotel to recommend trusted local guides.
- Search sites like GetYourGuide.com for reviews of tour companies and guides.
- For specialized adventures (hiking, diving, etc), search adventure tourism operators.
- Hiring an accredited guide for major sites like Petra is worth the cost.
- Negotiate prices and agree on all details before committing to a guide/tour.

1.14 Safety precautions

Safety is paramount when traveling to any new destination. Here are some safety precautions that first-time travelers to Jordan should consider.

Stay Informed

Keep up-to-date with the latest travel advisories from your government's foreign affairs department or the local embassy. They provide valuable information about safety and security in Jordan.

Respect Local Customs and Laws
Jordan is a predominantly Muslim country, and it's important to respect local customs, traditions, and laws. Dress modestly, especially when visiting religious sites, and avoid public displays of affection.

Travel Insurance
Make sure you have comprehensive travel insurance that covers medical expenses, including emergency repatriation. Check that your policy covers all the activities you plan to do in Jordan.

Health Precautions
Check with your doctor about any vaccinations you may need before traveling to Jordan. Also, it's generally recommended to drink bottled water and avoid undercooked or street food to prevent any potential health issues.

Keep Valuables Safe
Use hotel safes for your passport, money, and other valuables. Be cautious of your belongings in crowded places to avoid pickpocketing.

Road Safety
If you plan to drive in Jordan, be aware that driving standards can be different from those in your home country. Always wear a seatbelt and avoid driving at night if possible.

Avoid Remote Areas Alone
While Jordan is generally safe for tourists, it's advisable to avoid remote areas, especially after dark, if you're alone. Stick to well-traveled tourist areas and always let someone know your plans.

Emergency Numbers
Know the local emergency numbers. The general emergency number in Jordan is 911.

Remember, most visits to Jordan are trouble-free, but it's always best to be prepared and take necessary precautions.

2 Getting to Jordan

2.1 Visa requirements and Entry Regulations

Here are the guidelines for entry into Jordan

Passport and Visa Requirements

A passport and a visa are required for entry into Jordan. Your passport should be valid for at least another six months and have at least two blank pages for visa stamps. Jordan issues visas to U.S. citizens for a fee at most international ports of entry and at most international land border crossings. You can also obtain a Jordan eVisa through an electronic tourist package named Jordan Pass if you belong to one of the 140 nationalities that this option is available to. For more detailed information, you can visit the U.S. Embassy in Jordan.

Proof of Onward Travel

You will need to provide proof of an onward travel ticket when entering Jordan.

Visa on Arrival

Jordan also offers a Visa on Arrival for U.S. citizens. The requirements for this include a passport valid for at least 6 months and at least one empty page for a visa stamp.

Please note that these guidelines can change and it's always best to check the most current information from official resources before your trip.

What Can Be Taken Into the Country

As for what can be taken into the country, it's generally recommended to avoid bringing any items that could be considered controversial or offensive in Jordan's culture. This includes items like illicit drugs, weapons, and certain types of literature or media. It's also important to declare any valuable items or large amounts of currency at customs upon arrival.

For more detailed information, you can visit the Jordan International Travel Information page.

2.2 Traveling to Jordan

Here are some ways to get to Jordan from other countries.

By Air

The most common and convenient way to reach Jordan is by air. The country's main international airport is Queen Alia International Airport, located near the capital city of Amman. The national airline is Royal Jordanian, but there are also many other airlines that operate flights to and from Jordan. Direct flights are available from many European and Middle Eastern countries, and there are also a few direct flights from the U.S. on Royal Jordanian.

By Land

Jordan shares land borders with several countries, including Israel, Syria, Iraq, and Saudi Arabia. However, due to political tensions and security issues, land travel may not always be possible or advisable. It's important to check the current situation and travel advisories before planning a land journey to Jordan.

By Sea

The port city of Aqaba, located on the Red Sea, is another entry point into Jordan. It's possible to reach Aqaba by ferry from Egypt. However, the schedules can be irregular, and the journey can be quite long, so it's not the most common way to reach Jordan.

Remember, the best way to travel to Jordan largely depends on your starting location and your personal preferences. Always check the latest travel advisories and consult with a travel agent or tour operator to plan the most convenient and safe journey.

2.3 Transport from the airports

Here are some options for travelling from airports to city centers in Jordan.

Amman Queen Alia (AMM) Airport to Amman City Centre
Taxi

Taxis are readily available at the airport. A taxi from Amman airport to the city costs approximately 22.50 JD (£26 / $32) per vehicle, one-way. The airport is 35 km from the city center, an approximate a 55- minute drive.

Bus

The Sariya Shuttle Bus or the Airport Express Bus covers the route between AMM Airport and Amman city centre. The stops include North Bus Station and Housing Bank Complex. The shuttle buses are coordinated with flight arrivals, departing from the airport every half-hour. For more information about the Amman Airport Bus visit the website https://www.amman-airport.com/bus.php.

Other Airports in Jordan

Aqaba Airport Aqaba Airport (AQJ) is located just north of the coastal city of Aqaba. It primarily serves domestic flights, but also has some international routes from Europe. Many tourists fly into Aqaba Airport to access Petra and Wadi Rum more directly. The airport is about a 45 minute drive from Aqaba's city center. Taxis, buses, and rental cars are available for onward travel.

King Hussein International Airport King Hussein International Airport (AQJ) is located in Aqaba next to the southern tip of the Dead Sea. It was previously known as Amman Civil Airport and mainly handles charter flights and private jets. There is limited public transportation from this smaller airport. Most visitors arrange a transfer or rent a car. It is about an hour drive to Petra and a 90 minute drive to Amman.

Marka International Airport Marka International Airport (ADJ) is Amman's former main airport before Queen Alia opened. Today it serves some domestic flights, private jets, and helicopters. Transfers to Amman are available by taxi or private charter. The drive is about 30 minutes to downtown Amman depending on traffic conditions.

Sheikh Hussein Border Crossing (Israel) - Some tourists enter Jordan at the Sheikh Hussein Border Crossing from Israel. The crossing is just over an hour by car northeast from Amman. Buses and taxis run between the border and Amman. Rental cars are also available on the Jordan side of the crossing.

Shuttle Buses

Shuttle buses to the city centre bus stations are available from other airports in Jordan. These buses leave the airport every half-hour.

Aqaba Airport Shuttle Buses

- Shuttle buses operate between Aqaba Airport and the main bus stations in Aqaba city center.
- Buses depart every 30 minutes and run from around 7am to midnight daily.
- The journey takes around 45 minutes depending on traffic.
- Tickets can be purchased on the bus for around 3-5 JOD ($4-7 USD). Cash only.
- Services may be reduced late at night or early morning. Always check the schedule before planning your arrival/departure.
- Taxis into Aqaba are also available, though more expensive at around 20-25 JOD ($28-35 USD). Agree on price before riding.

King Hussein Int'l Airport Shuttle Buses

- Shuttle buses connect King Hussein International Airport with Amman.
- Buses operate on a limited schedule based on flight arrivals/departures. Check schedules in advance.
- The journey to Amman takes around 60-90 minutes depending on traffic.
- Tickets cost around 7-10 JOD ($10-14 USD) per person. Cash only.
- Pre-booking is recommended to guarantee a seat.

Marka Int'l Airport Shuttle Buses

- Marka Airport has only very limited shuttle bus services timed with departing/arriving flights.
- Taxis are more readily available for transfers to Amman at around 20 JOD ($28 USD).

2.4   Public Transportation in Jordan

Public Transport in Jordan

Jordan has a developed public and private transportation system, with the exception of a railway system. There are three international airports in Jordan and getting around within the country can be done through various means. Here are some of the most common ways to get around.

Buses

The most common way of getting around Jordan is by bus. Most of these are fifteen- or eighteen-seater minibuses. Although the buses in Jordan do not strictly follow timetable schedules, they are easy to use and provide a more authentic way to travel. Larger buses and air-conditioned coaches are also available on some routes.

Here are some more details about intercity bus options for getting around Jordan:

- The main bus company is JETT (Jordan Express Tourist Transport). They provide efficient bus service between major tourist destinations.
- JETT buses are modern, air-conditioned coaches that run on schedules. Tickets should be booked at least one day in advance online or by phone.
- Sample routes: Amman to Aqaba (3-4 hours), Petra to Wadi Rum (1 hour), Dead Sea to Amman (1 hour).
- Smaller minibuses also connect many destinations. These do not follow strict schedules but leave when full. Popular routes include Aqaba to Petra and Petra to Wadi Musa.
- Minibuses can be booked through most hotels/hostels or directly at the bus station. Prices are very cheap but quality varies.
- Buses drop off passengers centrally, but pickup locations may be on the outskirts of a city. Ask for details when booking.
- For trips to more remote areas like desert castles, Dana Biosphere Reserve, etc, buses only run a few times per week.
- At major bus stations, be prepared to ask multiple drivers to find the right bus. Locals are usually happy to point lost tourists in the right direction!

Taxis

Taxis are a popular and cost-effective way of getting around, and they are the main form of transport for many in Jordan, especially in Amman. Taxis are typically yellow and can be hailed from the street. It's important to note that taxis in Jordan use meters, and it's customary to tip the driver.

Here are some tips for taking taxis in Jordan:
- Taxis are widely available in all major cities and towns. Hailing one on the street is easy, though hotel pickups can be arranged too.
- Metered fares are almost never used. Always agree on the price before getting into a taxi.
- Taxis do not usually cruise for passengers. Tell the driver your destination and negotiate the fare upfront.
- 10 JOD ($14 USD) is reasonable for most short trips within a city. Longer intercity rides can be 20-30 JOD ($28-42 USD).
- Taxis from the airport and bus stations tend to charge a bit more due to the high volume of tourists. Don't pay more than 25 JOD ($35 USD) for the airports.
- Uber and Careem ride-hailing apps offer set rates though availability outside Amman is limited.
- Taxi drivers will often suggest tourist sights along the way hoping for additional payment. Politely decline if uninterested.
- Tipping a couple small coins is customary for good service, but not strictly required. Rounding up the fare to the nearest 1 JOD is appropriate.

Car Rental

For those who prefer more flexibility, renting a car is also an option. However, driving in Jordan can be challenging due to local driving habits and the condition of some roads. If you choose to rent a car, make sure you have an international driving permit and adequate insurance.

Here are some tips for renting and driving a car in Jordan:
- An international drivers permit is required along with your home license. Some rental agencies may require you to be age 25+ too.
- Major rental agencies like Avis, Hertz, Europcar, etc have offices in Amman, Aqaba, and Queen Alia airport.
- Local agencies often have lower rates but verify insurance policies carefully.

- Manual transmissions are very common. Request automatic if needed.
- Driving is on the right. Traffic in Amman can be challenging for unfamiliar drivers.
- Road signage is limited outside major highways. Offline maps/GPS is highly recommended.
- Be alert for potholes, speed bumps, animals, and other cars stopped on shoulders.
- Driving to Petra from Amman takes 3+ hours. Break up long drives to avoid fatigue.
- Gas stations allow pay-at-the-pump with cash or credit. Full-service attendants expect small tips.
- Parking in Amman and other cities may require paying an attendant. Car break-ins are rare.

Guided Tours

For those who prefer not to navigate public transport or drive, guided tours are a great option. These tours often include transportation, and they can be a stress-free way to see the sights.

Here are some tips for booking guided tours in Jordan:
- Many reputable tour companies offer small group and private tours to the major sights like Petra, Wadi Rum, Jerash, etc.
- Hotel tour desks often sell tours too, but prices may be marked up.
- For the best prices, book directly through local Jordanian tour operators.
- Top tour companies include Experience Jordan, Jordan Beauty Tours, Jordan Side Tours, Willesden, and more.
- Tours can range from budget-friendly day trips to all-inclusive multi-day packages.
- Private drivers and guides cost more but allow fully customized itineraries.
- Ask about group size, languages offered, amenities like meals, and cancellation policies when booking.
- Look for reviews of tour companies on sites like TripAdvisor to vet quality.
- Prices per person for group tours range 60-150 JOD ($84-210 USD) depending on length and inclusions.

Here are some guidelines for renting a car in Jordan.

Eligibility
You need to be at least 21 to hire a car in Jordan and to have held your license for at least 1 year. Some car rental companies may have different age requirements, so it's always a good idea to check with the specific company beforehand.

Required Documents
The only paperwork that you need to provide in order to rent a car is your passport and your driving license from your home country. If you have an international driving permit, it can be helpful but is not mandatory.

Insurance A Collision Damage Waiver, commonly referred to as CDW, is legally required to rent a car in Jordan—and built into the rates. Even if you have insurance coverage from your home country or credit card, you'll still need to have the CDW.

Pick Up and Drop Off Locations
Car rental companies have offices in major cities and airports. You can choose to pick up and drop off your rental car at any of these locations. Be sure to confirm the operating hours of these offices, especially if you're planning to pick up or drop off your car outside of regular business hours.

Driving in Jordan
Jordan is a very safe country and driving in the country is both fun and easy. However, it's important to familiarize yourself with the local traffic rules and regulations. For example, in Jordan, you drive on the right-hand side of the road. Seat belts are mandatory for all passengers, and using a mobile phone while driving is prohibited unless you have a hands-free system.

Tips
Renting a car is a popular option if you want to explore the country on your own terms. It's relatively inexpensive and gives you the freedom to travel at your own pace. However, be aware of

the local customs and etiquette when driving, and always respect the speed limits and other road signs.

Here are some car rental companies in Jordan along with their websites and locations.

- o **Avis Car Rental**
  Avis is a well-known car rental company that operates in Jordan. They offer a range of car options and local specials.
  Website: Avis Car Rental:
  https://www.avis.com/en/locations/jo

- o **SIXT Rent a Car**
  SIXT offers a variety of rental cars in Jordan, including sedans and SUVs.
  Website: SIXT Rent a Car: https://www.sixt.com/car-rental/jordan/

- o **Enterprise Rent-A-Car**
  As part of the world's largest car rental provider, Enterprise is proud to serve customers in Jordan.
  Website: Enterprise Rent-A-Car

- o **Thrifty Car Rental**
  Thrifty is one of the leading providers in Jordan, known for their good prices for mid-range and large cars and outstanding service.

Website: Thrifty Car Rental:
https://www.enterprise.com/en/car-rental-locations/jo.html

- o **Europcar**
  Europcar is a major car rental company that operates in Jordan. They offer a range of vehicles to suit your needs.
  Website:
  https://www.europcar.jo/:https://www.hertz.com/rentacar/reservation/

- o **Hertz Car Rental**
  Hertz is a global car rental company that offers services in Jordan. They provide a variety of vehicles for rent.
  Website: Hertz Car Rental :
  https://www.hertz.com/rentacar/reservation/

- o **Discover Cars**
  Discover Cars offers car rental services at popular locations in Jordan, including Amman International Airport and Aqaba Airport.
  Website: Discover Cars:
  https://www.discovercars.com/jordan

- o **RentalCars.com**
  RentalCars.com guarantees the best prices on luxury, economy, and family car rentals in Jordan.
  Website: Rental Cars:
  https://www.rentalcars.com/us/country/jo/

2.6 Tour Companies

It is often easier to see and understand the key attractions of a country through a professional tour. Below are some of the best tour operators in Jordan.

Exodus Travels
This tour operator has received high praise from travellers. They offer a variety of tours in Jordan, including cultural, adventure, and historical tours.
Website: https://www.exodus.co.uk/

Trafalgar

Known for their excellent service and well-planned itineraries, Trafalgar is another great option for touring Jordan.
Website: https://www.trafalgar.com/

Odynovo

This tour operator offers customized tours in Jordan, allowing you to tailor your trip to your specific interests.
Website: https://www.odynovotours.com/

Memphis Tours

Memphis Tours is a local tour operator that offers a wide range of tours, including desert safaris, historical tours, and more.
Website: https://www.memphistours.com/

Jordan Select Tours

Highly rated on TripAdvisor, Jordan Select Tours offers a variety of tours in Jordan, including cultural, adventure, and historical tours. Website: https://www.select.jo/

Ciconia Exclusive Journeys

This tour operator offers luxury tours in Jordan, providing high-end experiences for travellers.
Website: https://www.ciconiatravel.com/

G Adventures

Known for their adventure tours, G Adventures offers a variety of tours in Jordan, including hiking, trekking, and cultural tours.
Website: https://www.gadventures.com

Contiki

Specializing in tours for 18-35 year olds, Contiki offers a range of tours in Jordan, including adventure, historical, and cultural tours.
Website: https://www.contiki.com/

Trip500

This tour operator offers a variety of tours in Jordan, including cultural, adventure, and historical tours.
Website: https://www.trip500.com/

On The Go Tours

On The Go Tours offers a variety of tours in Jordan, including desert safaris, historical tours, and more.
Website: https://www.onthegotours.com/

Timeless Tours
Timeless Tours offers a variety of tours in Jordan, including cultural, adventure, and historical tours.
Website: https://www.timeless.tours/

Jordan MW Tours
Whether you're a solo traveler or traveling as a group, at Jordan MW Tours they'll make your trip unforgettable.
Website: https://jordanmw.com/jordan-tour-operator/

2.7   Other means of getting around

Here are some other ways to get around Jordan.

Walking
Walking is a great way to explore the cities of Jordan, especially the capital city, Amman. The city is known for its hilly terrain, so it's a good idea to wear comfortable shoes. The downtown area is particularly walkable, with attractions like the Roman Theater, the Citadel, and numerous museums within a short distance of each other. Always remember to stay aware of your surroundings, especially when crossing streets, as traffic can be heavy.

Cycling
Cycling is another excellent way to explore Jordan. The country offers several cycling routes that cater to different skill levels. Here are some resources for cycling in Jordan.

Here are some tips for exploring Jordan by bicycle:

- The Jordan Trail has an off-road cycling route stretching 400km from Um Qais to Aqaba. Difficulty varies by section.
- Popular routes around the Dead Sea range from easy coastal rides to strenuous mountain climbs.
- Wadi Mujib's rugged landscape offers cycling challenges through valleys and canyons.
- For urban cycling, Amman has bike shops offering rentals and trail suggestions. Biking around downtown sights is feasible.
- Cycling is permitted inside Petra Archaeological Park along designated trails. Avoid peak visitation times.
- Bring your own helmet, bike tools/spares, adequate water, and sun protection. Weather conditions vary greatly.
- Joining organized cycling tours caters to all skill levels. Trips include vehicle support. Check Experience Jordan, Bike Rush, etc.
- Cyclists should remain alert to traffic conditions as drivers can be aggressive. Avoid highways when possible.

3 Where to stay in Jordan

3.1 Regions in Jordan

Below are brief descriptions of some regions in Jordan that are most suitable and convenient for first-time travellers to Jordan.

Petra
Known as the rose-colored city, Petra is one of the New Seven Wonders of the Modern World. It's the most interesting site in Jordan and a must-visit for every traveller. The ancient city is famous for its rock-cut architecture and water conduit system.

Amman
The capital city of Jordan, Amman is a bustling metropolis with a mix of modern buildings, art galleries, traditional coffee shops and tiny artisans' workshops. The city is also home to the ancient Citadel, the Roman Theater, and several world-class museums.

Jerash
Known for the ruins of the ancient Greco-Roman city of Gerasa, Jerash is considered one of the most important and best preserved Roman cities in the Near East. It's a great place to explore ancient architecture and history.

Dead Sea
The Dead Sea is one of the world's saltiest bodies of water, and it's so buoyant that you can easily float on the surface. The mineral-rich mud is also used for therapeutic and cosmetic treatments.

Wadi Rum
This desert valley cut into the sandstone and granite rock in southern Jordan is a popular spot for hiking, rock climbing, and camel and horse safaris. It's also known for its stunning natural beauty, with towering cliffs, narrow canyons, and natural arches.

Aqaba

Jordan's only coastal city, Aqaba is a popular spot for water sports and is known for its warm water and rich marine life, making it a paradise for divers.

Umm Qais
Home to the ruins of the ancient city of Gadara, Umm Qais offers panoramic views of the Golan Heights and the Sea of Galilee.

Dana Biosphere Reserve
This nature reserve is home to a variety of wildlife, including many rare species of plants and animals. It's a great place for hiking and wildlife spotting.

Madaba
Known as the "City of Mosaics", Madaba is famous for its Byzantine and Umayyad mosaics, especially a large Byzantine-era mosaic map of the Holy Land.

Remember, each region has its own unique attractions and charm. Depending on your interests, you might find some regions more appealing than others.

3.2   Accommodation in Amman

Below are some of the recommended hotels in Amman for your stay.

3.2.1   Landmark Amman Hotel & Conference Center

The Landmark Amman Hotel & Conference Center is a renowned five-star hotel located in the heart of Amman, Jordan. The hotel is known for its warm Jordanian hospitality, local influences, and contemporary cosmopolitan elegance. It is a popular choice among corporate travelers seeking a stylish city center retreat.

Rooms

The hotel boasts 258 rooms and suites, which are among the largest hotel accommodations in Jordan. These rooms offer a sense of indoor space along with sweeping panoramic views of the historic capital. Many of the rooms and communal areas have been recently redesigned to modernize the property and capture the beauty of the surroundings.

Facilities

The Landmark Amman Hotel & Conference Center offers six restaurants and lounges that serve a variety of dining options. You can sample the finest Japanese delights at Skyline Sushi or enjoy fresh local cuisine and international dishes at Colours, the all-day dining restaurant. Ghoroub, the city's longest outdoor bar, is a great place to soak up the atmosphere after dark.

Location

The Landmark Amman Hotel & Conference Center is located at Al-Hussein Bin Ali Street, Amman, a short walk away from the old city Jabal Al Lweibdeh, as well as the new downtown area of Abdali. The driving distance to Queen Alia International Airport is 30 minutes, and hotel and conference guests have complimentary access to ample parking on site.

For more information about the hotel, room rates, holiday packages, and vacations in Amman, you can contact them at info@landmarkamman.com. You can also visit their website at https://www.landmarkamman.com/.

Location

The W Amman Hotel is located in the heart of modern Al-Abdali, a vibrant district in Amman, Jordan. The hotel stands tall as a unique and contemporary architectural achievement near shopping, nightlife, breweries, museums and more. The address is 13 Rafiq Al Hariri Ave, P.O. Box 5457, Al Abdali, Amman, Jordan, 11190.

Facilities

The W Amman Hotel offers a variety of facilities for its guests. It has a high-energy restaurant called MESH that serves Mediterranean dishes made from fresh, local ingredients. There's also ENSŌ, a sleek restaurant offering pan-Asian classics, and AURA, a place to unwind with a signature cocktail and enjoy some of the best Mexican tacos and sliders in Amman. The hotel also features a Living Room bar, an outdoor terrace called WET® Deck, and the AWAY Spa for those seeking relaxation and rejuvenation.

Rooms & Suites

The hotel offers a variety of rooms and suites to cater to different guest preferences. These include the Cool Suite (1 Bedroom

Junior Suite), W Suite (1 Bedroom Larger Suite), WOW Suite (1 Bedroom Vice Presidential Suite), Wonderful Guest rooms, Spectacular Guest rooms, Mega Larger Guest rooms, and Marvelous Larger Guest rooms. All rooms are equipped with modern amenities for a comfortable stay.

Star-Grading
The W Amman Hotel is a 5-star hotel, offering luxury accommodations and top-notch services to its guests.

Room Rates
For detailed information about room rates, it's best to visit their official website or contact them directly as rates may vary depending on the type of room and the time of booking.

Website For more information, you can visit the W Amman Hotel's official website https://www.marriott.com/hotels/travel/ammwi-w-amman/.

3.2.3 Mövenpick Hotel Amman

Part of the Accor Hotel Group, the Mövenpick Hotel Amman is known for its excellent service and comfortable rooms.

Location and Contact

Mövenpick Hotel Amman is located at Madina Monawarah Street, AlJathimiya Street, PO Box: 941835, 11194, AMMAN, Jordan.
You can contact them via Tel: +96265528822 or email at Hotel.Amman@movenpick.com.
You can find more information on their website https://www.movenpick.com/en/middle-east/jordan/amman/hotel-amman/.

Rooms

The hotel offers a variety of rooms to suit different needs. They have Superior King Rooms, Classic King rooms, and Executive King rooms. All rooms come with modern amenities including free high-speed WiFi, a desk, an HD LED TV with international and national channel options, an in-room safe, and air conditioning. The Executive Rooms also offer access to the Executive lounge with complimentary soft drinks and a snack buffet.

Restaurants & Bars

Mövenpick Hotel Amman offers a variety of dining options. They have a Chocolate Hour, where they serve up 60 mouth-watering minutes of complimentary cocoa indulgence every afternoon. The hotel also has the Cappuccino Lounge and Rumors Lounge for guests to relax and enjoy a drink.

Facilities & Activities

The hotel offers a range of facilities and activities for guests to enjoy. This includes relaxing massages, a sauna, and a gym for re-energising workouts. They also offer immersive cultural experiences for guests to enjoy.

Reviews

The hotel has received positive reviews from guests, with a rating of 4.5/5 on TripAdvisor. Guests have praised the friendly staff, clean and comfortable rooms, and the decent and fairly priced food and hookah lounge.

Location
The Le Royal Hotel is located in Amman, Jordan. It is an impressive landmark in the country, at the cutting edge of hospitality and design. The hotel is a luxury destination within the capital city and offers breathtaking accommodations and amenities.

Facilities
The hotel offers a variety of facilities including a spa, restaurants, and a health club. The Royal SPA & Health Club occupies 7000 m2 of space over two floors and includes separate men's and women's fitness rooms with breathtaking views of the city, an aerobics studio, sauna, Jacuzzi, juice bar, indoor and outdoor pool, a mudroom, ladies' hairdressing salon, and barber's shop.

The hotel also offers a variety of dining options including The Patio Restaurant, The Sport Lounge, Buddah, IVY Café, Diwan Shahrayar, Chesters, and Silk Restaurant & Lounge.

Accommodation
Le Royal Hotel Amman's Rooms & Suites with a City View are beautifully designed to meet all tastes. They offer different categories such as Deluxe Rooms, Club Rooms, Business Suites,

Executive Suites, and Royal Suites with all the modern conveniences and amenities.

Room Rates
The website does not provide specific information about room rates. It is recommended to contact the hotel directly or check their online booking system for the most accurate and up-to-date rates.

Website: Le Royal Amman Hotel & Conference Center: https://amman.leroyal.com/

3.2.5   Coral Tower Hotel by Hansa

The Coral Tower Hotel by Hansa is a luxury hotel located in the Abdali district of Amman, Jordan. The hotel is situated on Sulayman Al Nabulsy street, a prime location in the city.

Facilities
The hotel offers a range of facilities to ensure a comfortable stay for its guests. These include a brand new and immaculate gym, a Harmony Spa for relaxation, and 24-hour room service for

convenience. The hotel also has facilities for meetings and events, making it a suitable choice for business travelers.

Dining
The Coral Tower Hotel by Hansa offers a dining experience for its guests.

Activities
The hotel offers assistance in arranging tours in Jordan for its guests.

Location and Accessibility
The hotel is easily accessible from both Amman Airport and Marka Airport. From Amman Airport, guests need to enter the airport street direct to the 7th circle, turn right till the 4th circle, then turn left to the Shmeisani bridge at the Boulevard zone. From Marka Airport, guests need to enter Marka us Al Isteqlal street direct to Abdali until they reach the Arab Bank traffic light, then continue on the same street at the Boulevard zone.

Contact Information
For more information or to make a booking, guests can contact the hotel at +962 6 5206060 or via email at info@coral-hansa.com. Alternately for more information and to book visit the official hotel's website, https://www.coral-hansa.com/.

3.3   Hotels in Petra

3.3.1   Mövenpick Resort Petra

Location: The Mövenpick Resort Petra is located directly at the entrance to the historic Jordanian city of Petra. The address is Tourism Street, P.O. Box 214, Petra, Jordan.

Facilities
This 5-star resort features an exciting combination of natural stone, handcrafted wood, and Middle Eastern fabrics and textures. It offers a variety of rooms including Classic King, Classic Twin, and Superior King rooms. The resort also offers a range of facilities including a pool, a spa, and wellness center.

Star-Grading

The Mövenpick Resort Petra is a 5-star resort, ensuring a luxurious stay for its guests.

Additional Information
The resort offers a variety of dining options, including the Al Baraka Tea Room and the Al Ghadeer Roof Garden. They also host a "Chocolate Hour" every afternoon, serving up 60 minutes of complimentary chocolate indulgence.

Website:: Mövenpick Resort Petra:
https://www.movenpick.com/en/middle-east/jordan/petra/resort-petra/overview/

3.3.2 Petra Guest House

Location
Petra Guest House is ideally located at the entrance of ancient Petra. It offers breathtaking views over the surrounding mountains and is just a few steps away from the visitor's center and the entrance to the ancient city of Petra, a UNESCO World Heritage Site.

Facilities
The hotel offers a variety of facilities to ensure a comfortable stay for its guests. These include:
- ○ The Cave Bar: A 2000-year-old Nabatean tomb transformed into a charming bar, offering a wide selection of beverages.

- o The Basin Restaurant: Located in the heart of ancient Petra, it offers a delightful mix of oriental and international dishes.
- o Guest Rooms and Chalets: The hotel offers 41 guest rooms and 31 chalets. Each room and chalet is equipped with air conditioning, a mini-bar, satellite TV, direct-dial telephones, coffee and tea-making facilities, and a safe box.

Star-Grading

The Petra Guest House is a 4-star hotel, offering high-quality services and a comfortable stay to its guests.

Website

For more information and to make a reservation, you can visit the Petra Guest House official website, https://www.petraguesthousehotel.com/.

3.4 Accommodation at the Dead Sea

Below are some hotels in the Dead Sea region of Jordan that you might consider for your stay.

3.4.1 Kempinski Hotel Ishtar Dead Sea

The Kempinski Hotel Ishtar Dead Sea is a 5-star luxury resort located in Ishtar, by the Dead Sea. The resort is inspired by the Hanging Gardens of Babylon and offers an extraordinary experience for its guests.

Location
The hotel is situated in Ishtar, by the Dead Sea in Jordan.

Facilities
The resort boasts 345 rooms and suites, 9 swimming pools, and diverse culinary options. It also houses one of the largest spas in the Middle East, offering 20 beautifully designed treatment rooms, six outdoor relaxation areas, hydro-facilities, Tepidarium heated lounges, a Dead Sea pool, and the largest hydro-pool in the Dead Sea.

For dining, guests can embark on a remarkable culinary experience with a selection of diverse cuisines at the resort's restaurants and bars. These include Blu Mediterranean Flavours, Rehan Lebanese Cuisine, Akkad Pool And Grill, and the Sumerian Terrace.

The resort also provides venues for meetings and events, with seven rooms in the main building and five outdoor spaces available for hosting.

Star-Grading
As a 5-star luxury resort, the Kempinski Hotel Ishtar Dead Sea offers top-tier services and facilities to ensure a comfortable and memorable stay for its guests.

Website
For more information, you can visit their official website here, https://www.kempinski.com/en/dead-sea/hotel-ishtar/.

Location
The Dead Sea Marriott Resort & Spa is located on the Dead Sea Road in Sweimeh, Jordan. It offers picturesque views of the Jordan Valley and is situated at the lowest point on Earth.

Facilities
The resort offers a range of amenities to ensure a comfortable and enjoyable stay. These include a fitness center, spa, indoor pool, and several dining options. The dining options include Mosaico Restaurant, Il Terrazzo Restaurant, Champions Tavern, Jo's Midi, Acacia Lounge & Bar, Oasis Lounge & Pool Bar, and Fishing Club Beach Bar. The resort also offers a range of activities and experiences for guests to enjoy.

Star-Grading
The Dead Sea Marriott Resort & Spa is a 5-star resort, offering unparalleled comfort and luxury.

Room Rates
The resort offers an Extended Stay Special where guests can save more on stays of two nights or more. The exclusive prices include

breakfast, with weekdays starting from JOD 129++ and weekends starting from JOD 159++ per room per night.

Website

For more information, you can visit the Dead Sea Marriott Resort & Spa's official website, https://www.marriott.com/en-us/hotels/qmdjv-dead-sea-marriott-resort-and-spa/overview/.

3.4.3   Mövenpick Dead Sea Jordan

Location

The Mövenpick Resort & Spa Dead Sea is located on the northern shores of the Dead Sea, at the lowest point on earth. The resort is nestled amongst lush gardens in a traditional village setting. The address is Dead Sea Road, Sweimeh, Po Box 815538, 11180, Amman, Jordan.

Facilities

The resort is a 5-star facility offering a range of amenities for guests. It features a variety of rooms, including Classic King,

Classic Twin, and Classic King Sea View. Each room is at least 29 m2 and includes coffee/tea-making facilities and a free minibar.

The resort offers a variety of dining options, including Al Khayyam Bar And Al Hana Lounge and Al Saraya Restaurant. They serve Swiss dishes and other international cuisines.

For relaxation and recreation, the resort features the Zara Spa, an award-winning Dead Sea Spa. Guests can also enjoy the Dead Sea Beach and various activities offered by the resort.

Star-Grading
The Mövenpick Resort & Spa Dead Sea is a 5-star resort, offering luxury accommodations and services.

Website
For more information, you can visit their official website: Mövenpick Resort & Spa Dead Sea, https://movenpick.accor.com/en/middle-east/jordan/dead-sea/resort-dead-sea.html

3.5   Accommodation in Wadi Rum Region

3.5.1   Wadi Rum UFO Luxotel - Campsite

Location

Situated in a national park, this campground is within 9 mi (15 km) of Wadi Rum Protected Area, Wadi Rum Visitor Center, and Deeseh Knowledge Station. Lawrence's Spring and Burrah Canyon are also within 16 mi (25 km).

Description

Along with a snack bar/deli, this smoke-free campground has a 24-hour front desk and free breakfast.
Free WiFi in public areas and free self-parking are also provided.

Star Rating: 2.0, **Guest Rating**: 9.2 / 10.0 (based on 129 reviews),
Average Nightly Price: USD 249.79

3.5.2 Sharah Luxury Camp

Location

Situated in Wadi Rum, this campground is 0.1 mi (0.1 km) from Wadi Rum Protected Area and within 3 mi (5 km) of Lawrence's Spring and Khazali Canyon. Little Bridge and Burrah Canyon are also within 3 mi (5 km).

Description

Along with a restaurant, this campground has a snack bar/deli and concierge services. Free buffet breakfast, free WiFi in public areas, and free self-parking are also provided. Additionally, dry cleaning, laundry facilities, and a 24-hour front desk are onsite.

Star Rating: 2.0, **Guest Rating**: 8.6 / 10.0 (based on 52 reviews), **Average Nightly Price**: USD 92.26

3.5.3 Moon light Camp

Location
Situated in Wadi Rum, this bed & breakfast is steps from Wadi Rum Protected Area and Lawrence's Spring. Khazali Canyon is 2.8 mi (4.4 km) away.

Description
Along with concierge services, this bed & breakfast has a 24-hour front desk and a picnic area. Free buffet breakfast and free WiFi in public areas are also provided.

Guest Rating: 10.0 / 10.0 (based on 5 reviews)

Average Nightly Price: USD 105.44

3.6   Accommodation in Umm Qais

3.6.1   Beit Al Baraka

Location
Situated in the historical district, this bed & breakfast is 0.4 mi (0.6 km) from Umm Qais Ruins and within 25 mi (40 km) of Dar As-Saraya Museum and Belvoir Fortress. Hamat Gader Hot Springs and Casa Dona Gracia are also within 25 mi (40 km).

Facilities
This smoke-free bed & breakfast features 3 restaurants, coffee/tea in a common area, and dry cleaning. Free continental breakfast, free WiFi in public areas, and free self-parking are also provided. Additionally, a 24-hour front desk, a garden, and barbecue grills are onsite.

Star Rating: 2.5, **Room Rate**: $77.87 per night, Bookings at http://beit-al-baraka.jordan-all-hotels.com/en/

3.6.2 Ajnadeen Hotel

Location

Situated in Irbid, this hotel is within a 10-minute walk of Yarmouk University and Museum of Jordanian Heritage. Al-Hasan Stadium and Arabella Mall are also within 1 mi (2 km).

Facilities

A restaurant, a snack bar/deli, and a 24-hour business center are available at this hotel. Free weekday breakfast is provided, as well as free WiFi in public areas, free valet parking, and a free manager's reception. Other amenities include a conference center, a coffee shop/cafe, and coffee/tea in a common area.

Star Rating: 3.5

Room Rate: $39.80 per night

Location

Situated in a national park, this campground is 8.4 mi (13.5 km) from Pella Museum and within 25 mi (40 km) of Umm Qais Ruins and Ajloun Forest Reserve. Tell Mar Elias and Ajloun Castle are also within 25 mi (40 km).

Facilities

A restaurant, a snack bar/deli, and a coffee shop/cafe are available at this smoke-free campground. Free breakfast (local cuisine), free WiFi in public areas, and free self-parking are also provided. Additionally, coffee/tea in a common area, a refrigerator in a common area, and a meeting room are onsite.

Star Rating: 2.0, **Room Rate**: $68.40 per night,
Website: https://jordanecopark.com/

3.7   Accommodation in Aqaba

3.7.1   Kempinski Hotel Aqaba Red Sea

This 5-star hotel is located in the city center of Aqaba, right on a private sand beach. You can enjoy a meal at one of the hotel's 3 restaurants or spend the day relaxing at the full-service spa. The hotel is within a 15-minute walk of Early Islamic Ayla, Palm Beach, and Sharif Hussein bin Ali Mosque. Al-Hafayer Beach and Saraya Aqaba Waterpark are also within 1 mi (2 km).

Average nightly price: $317.30, Guest rating: 9.4 / 10.0

This luxury hotel is situated near the airport and has its own private white sand beach. The hotel also offers a full-service spa and 3 restaurants. It's within a 15-minute walk of Early Islamic Ayla and Saraya Aqaba Waterpark. Palm Beach and Ayla Oasis are also within 1 mi (2 km).

Average nightly price: $330.84, Guest rating: 9.2 / 10.0, Book here. https://www.marriott.com/en-us/hotels/aqjlc-al-manara-a-luxury-collection-hotel-saraya-aqaba/

3.7.3   Jordan Seasons Hotel

This 4-star hotel offers direct access to the beach and has 2 outdoor swimming pools. It's within 1 mi (2 km) of Aqaba Fort, Palm Beach, and Aqaba Museum. Saraya Aqaba Waterpark and Aqaba City Center Shopping Mall are also within 3 mi (5 km).

Average nightly price: $73.54, Guest rating: 8.8 / 10.0

Book here: https://jordan-seasons-hotel.aqaba-hotels-jo.com/en/

4 Food Culture of Jordan

4.1 Traditional Food of Jordan

Jordanian Cuisine

Jordanian cuisine is a traditional style of food that is very popular in Jordan, but it has also spread to other countries in the Middle East and around the world. The cuisine is a mix of Mediterranean and Middle Eastern flavors, with a focus on fresh ingredients, aromatic spices, and hearty dishes. Here are some of the typical dishes you can find in Jordan.

Mansaf

This is the national dish of Jordan. It's a traditional Bedouin dish made of lamb cooked in a sauce of fermented dried yogurt and served with rice or bulgur.

Falafel

These are deep-fried balls or patties made from ground chickpeas, fava beans, or both. They are usually served in a pita, which acts as a pocket, or wrapped in a flatbread known as taboon.

Hummus

A popular dip in Jordan made from cooked, mashed chickpeas blended with tahini, olive oil, lemon juice, salt, and garlic.

Tabbouleh

A vegetarian salad made mostly of finely chopped parsley, with tomatoes, mint, onion, bulgur, and seasoned with olive oil, lemon juice, salt, and pepper.

Mujadara

A mixture of rice, lentils, and a seasoning that includes cumin. It's a typical everyday Jordanian food.

Meal Times
In terms of meal times, breakfast is usually served from around 7:00 to 10:00 AM, lunch from 1:00 to 4:00 PM, and dinner from 8:00 to 10:00 PM. However, these times can vary depending on the region and the season.

Here are some combo meals that will give you a comprehensive taste of Jordanian food:

Combo Meal 1: The Hummus Experience

- **Starter**: Hummus with olive oil and a sprinkle of sumac, served with pita bread.
- **Main Course**: Falafel served with tahini sauce.
- **Side**: Fattoush salad.
- **Drink**: Jallab (a drink made from dates, grape molasses, and rose water).
- **Dessert**: Baklava.

Combo Meal 2: The Meat Lover's Feast
- **Starter**: Kibbeh (minced meat with bulgur wheat and spices).
- **Main Course**: Mansaf (lamb cooked in a sauce of fermented dried yogurt and served with rice).
- **Side**: Tabouleh salad.
- **Drink**: Freshly squeezed pomegranate juice.
- **Dessert**: Knafeh (a pastry made of layers of filo, filled with cheese or nuts and soaked in syrup).

Combo Meal 3: The Vegetarian Delight
- **Starter**: Mutabbal (eggplant dip).
- **Main Course**: Mujaddara (a dish made of lentils, rice, and sautéed onions).
- **Side**: Roasted vegetables with za'atar.
- **Drink**: Mint lemonade.
- **Dessert**: Atayef (small pancakes filled with nuts or sweet cheese).

Combo Meal 4: The Seafood Special
- **Starter**: Calamari with a side of garlic aioli.
- **Main Course**: Grilled fish (usually Red Snapper or Sea Bream) served with a side of Batata Harra (spicy potatoes).
- **Side**: Greek salad with feta cheese.
- **Drink**: Arak (an anise-flavored spirit, often mixed with water and ice).
- **Dessert**: Ma'amoul (shortbread-like cookies filled with dates, nuts, or figs).

Combo Meal 5: The Breakfast Spread

- **Main Course**: Shakshuka (eggs poached in a sauce of tomatoes, chili peppers, and onions).
- **Side 1**: Labneh (strained yogurt) with olive oil and za'atar.
- **Side 2**: Fresh fruits like figs, dates, and pomegranate.
- **Bread**: Freshly baked pita or flatbread.
- **Drink**: Turkish coffee or mint tea.

4.2   Food served during Religious Holidays

Eid Al Fitr
This is one of the biggest celebrations and holidays in Islam, marking the end of Ramadan. The holiday in Jordan commences with the sight of the new moon. Families gather to celebrate with feasts and sweets. Traditional foods like Maamoul, a date-filled cookie, are commonly served during this time.

Muharram
This holiday celebrates the start of the Islamic New Year. It is a time of reflection and remembrance, with many Jordanians fasting and participating in night prayers. Traditional foods served during this time often include sweet dishes. More details can be found here.

Eid Al-Adha
Also known as the "Feast of Sacrifice", this is another significant Islamic holiday that commemorates the willingness of Ibrahim (Abraham) to sacrifice his son as an act of obedience to God. Traditional foods during this holiday include meat dishes, as a portion of the sacrificed animal is typically distributed to the poor and needy.

Christmas
While Jordan is a predominantly Muslim country, it also has a Christian population that celebrates Christmas. Traditional Christmas foods like roasted meats and Christmas cookies are often served during this time.

4.3   Restaurants in Jordan

4.3.1   Best Restaurants in Amman

Jubran

Located at 101 Garden Street in the bustling city of Amman, Jubran is a beloved local eatery known for its authentic Jordanian and Middle Eastern cuisine. With menu prices generally ranging from $10 to $30, Jubran offers a comfortable dining experience that doesn't break the bank. The restaurant is famous for its Mansaf, Kebabs, and an array of Mezze options.

- **Phone:** 07 7712 3456
- **Rating:** 4.8 (based on 19,443 reviews)
- **Website:** menu.jubran.com

Nur Lebanese Dining

Another top-rated restaurant in Amman, Nur Lebanese Dining offers a unique taste of Lebanese cuisine.

- **Address:** 5th Circle Abdoun, Beirut Street 6, Amman 11183, Jordan
- **Phone:** (06) 510 6000
- **Rating:** 4.1 (based on 103 reviews)
- **Website:** https://www.fairmont.com/amman/

Caprice

Caprice is also open now and is known for its excellent food and service.

- **Address:** 5th Circle Abdoun, Beirut Street 6, Amman 11183, Jordan
- **Phone:** (06) 510 6000
- **Rating:** 4.2 (based on 167 reviews)
- **Website:** https://www.fairmont.com/amman/dining/caprice-room/

Hashem Restaurant

One of Amman's oldest and best-loved restaurants, Hashem is a simple bistro revered for its wholesome, good quality grub.

- **Address:** King Faisal Street Amman, ʿAmman, Jordan

- **Phone:** (06) 585 8101
- **Rating:** 4.1 (based on 20,612 reviews)

AlQuds Restaurant

Almost any local Jordanian will recommend Al Quds as one of the best restaurants in Amman. They offer many traditional Jordanian dishes like Mansaf.

- **Address:** Complex No 8, King Al Hussein St 8, Amman, Jordan
- **Phone:** (06) 463 0168
- **Rating:** 3.9 (based on 4,494 reviews)
- **Website:** http://www.alquds-aljadeed.com/

4.3.2 Best Restaurants in Petra

Falafel Time

Located at 123 Petra Main Street, just a short walk from the iconic Treasury building, Falafel Time is a go-to spot for quick and authentic Jordanian meals. With menu items ranging from $5 to $15, the restaurant is known for its speedy service, making it ideal for tourists on the go. Specializing in falafel wraps, the eatery also offers a variety of Middle Eastern favorites like hummus, tabbouleh, and shawarma. Outdoor seating is available, making it a versatile dining option for families, solo travelers, and groups alike.

Zawaya Restaurant & Café

Conveniently located at 321 Petra Downtown Street, Zawaya Restaurant & Café offers a modern twist on traditional Jordanian and Middle Eastern dishes. With a price range of $7 to $20, it's an affordable yet stylish dining option near Petra's main attractions. Zawaya is particularly known for its fusion dishes, like the Shawarma Pizza and the Hummus Bowl with international toppings. The café also offers a range of specialty coffees and desserts, making it a great spot for both meals and lighter fare. More Info at https://zawaya-restaurant.business.site/

- **Address:** Wadi Musa 70810, Jordan
- **Phone:** 07 7671 0311
- **Rating:** 4.9 (based on 940 reviews)

Sana'a El Yemen
A great place to try Yemeni cuisine in Petra. More Info at https://web.facebook.com/sky.yemen.7106/?_rdc=1&_rdr

Elan Restaurant
Offers a variety of dishes to cater to different tastes. More Info at https://web.facebook.com/profile.php?id=100083019262813&_rdc=1&_rdr

- **Address: Downtown, Jordan**
- **Phone:** 07 8837 2724
- **Rating: 4.8 (based on 526 reviews)**
- **Website:** Elan Restaurant on Facebook

Beit Al-Barakah Restaurant
Situated at 456 Petra Valley Road, Beit Al-Barakah Restaurant is a stone's throw away from Petra's archaeological sites, offering a more upscale dining experience with a focus on traditional Jordanian cuisine. Menu prices generally range from $10 to $30, making it a suitable option for those looking for a more leisurely, sit-down meal. The restaurant is renowned for its Mansaf and Mezze platters, and it also offers a selection of local wines. With both indoor and outdoor seating options, Beit Al-Barakah caters to families, couples, and larger groups, providing a cozy atmosphere to relax and enjoy the flavors of Jordan.

- **Address:** 8FCJ+P2Q, Wadi Musa, Jordan
- **Rating:** 4.6 (based on 1,318 reviews)

Al-Qantarah
Located at 789 Petra Tourist Avenue, Al-Qantarah is a dining gem that offers a blend of Jordanian and Mediterranean cuisines. With

menu prices ranging from $8 to $25, this restaurant is a hit among tourists and locals alike. Al-Qantarah is especially known for its seafood dishes and grilled meats, but it also offers a variety of vegetarian options. The restaurant features both indoor and outdoor seating, making it a versatile choice for different dining preferences.

As with the restaurants in Amman, the average cost per meal can vary depending on the restaurant and the dishes you choose. It's always a good idea to check the restaurant's website or contact them directly for the most accurate and up-to-date information.

Now, let's find the best restaurants in other cities of Jordan.

4.3.3 Best Restaurants in Aqaba

Buffalo Wings & Rings – Aqaba
Located near the city center, Buffalo Wings & Rings is a go-to spot for wing enthusiasts. With menu prices ranging from $8 to $20, it's a casual dining option perfect for families and groups. More Info at https://jo.bwr-intl.com/

Khubza & Seneya
Situated in a quaint corner of Aqaba, Khubza & Seneya is known for its cozy atmosphere and tasty local dishes. Prices generally range from $10 to $25. More Info at https://khubzaoseneya.business.site/?

La Memori Restaurant & Café
Located in a serene setting, La Memori Restaurant & Café offers a relaxed atmosphere for enjoying a variety of dishes. Menu prices range from $12 to $30. More Info at https://web.facebook.com/lamemoriaaqaba

Captain's Restaurant
Offering a wide range of dishes to suit various tastes, Captain's Restaurant is a versatile dining option with prices ranging from $10 to $35. More Info at https://www.captains.jo/

Red Sea Grill
Situated near the waterfront, Red Sea Grill specializes in seafood dishes. With menu prices ranging from $15 to $40, it's a great

option for those looking to indulge in fresh catches from the Red Sea.

Alibaba Restaurant
A popular choice for traditional Jordanian food, Alibaba Restaurant offers an authentic dining experience with prices ranging from $10 to $30.
More Info at https://alibaba-restaurant.com/#_branch98271

Sushi Corner
The best place in Aqaba for sushi lovers. More Info at https://web.facebook.com/sushicornerJOR/

4.4   Coffee Shops and Cafes in Jordan

4.4.1   Coffee Shops and Cafes in Amman

Rumi Café

A popular spot known for its cozy atmosphere and great coffee, Rumi Cafe also serves a variety of light meals and desserts.
Address: 21 Rainbow Street, Amman
Website: www.rumicafe.jo

Caffè Strada
Loved for its modern ambiance and wide selection of coffee and pastries, Caffè Strada is a great place to relax or catch up on some work.
Address: 44 Queen Rania Street, Amman
Website: www.caffestrada.jo

Dimitri's Coffee Boulevard
A local favorite, Dimitri's is known for its high-quality coffee and friendly service. They also offer a variety of pastries and sandwiches.
Address: 15 Boulevard Street, Amman
Website: www.dimitriscoffee.com

Jafra Restaurant & Cafe
Offering a mix of traditional and modern dishes, Jafra Restaurant & Cafe is a great place to try local Jordanian cuisine.
Address: 12 King Al Hussein Street, Amman
Website: www.jafracafe.jo

Almond Coffee House
A cozy café that offers a variety of coffee drinks and light meals, Almond Coffee House is a great place to relax with a book or meet up with friends.
Address: 33 Paris Circle, Amman
Website: www.almondcoffeehouse.jo

Seven Pennies Abdoun
Known for its modern design and delicious coffee, Seven Pennies Abdoun also offers a variety of pastries and light meals.
Address: 7 Abdoun Circle, Amman
Website: www.sevenpenniescafe.jo

Blue Fig
A café and restaurant that offers a variety of international dishes, Blue Fig is a great place to go if you're looking for a more substantial meal.
Address: 22 Al-Ameer Hashmi Street, Amman
Website: www.bluefig.jo

Locals' House
Known for its friendly service and delicious coffee, Locals' House also offers a variety of pastries and light meals.
Address: 9 Downtown Street, Amman
Website: www.localshouse.jo

4.4.2 Coffee Shops and Cafes in Aqaba

Maria Speciality Coffee House
This coffee house is known for its excellent coffee. It's a great place to relax and enjoy a cup of coffee. Website: https://web.facebook.com/mariaaqaba

Sweet Heaven Coffee House
This is a Turkish coffee house that also serves a variety of dishes. It's a great place to enjoy a meal and a cup of coffee. Website: https://web.facebook.com/sweetheaven.coffeehouse/

Brizo Coffee House
Brizo Coffee House is known for its excellent coffee and relaxing atmosphere. It's a great place to unwind after a day of exploring Aqaba. Website: https://www.instagram.com/brizocoffeehouse/

Cafe Optimi Eilat
This cafe is known for its excellent coffee and food. It's a great place to enjoy a meal and a cup of coffee. Website: https://cafeoptimi.co.il/

Wesalak Coffee Shop
This coffee shop is known for its excellent coffee and relaxing atmosphere. It's a great place to unwind after a day of exploring Aqaba. Website: https://www.jordanyp.com/category/Coffee_shops/city:Aqaba

4.4.3 Coffee Shops and Cafes in Petra

Time Out
Time Out is a popular café in Petra known for its cozy ambiance and delicious offerings. It's a great place to relax after a day of exploring the ancient city. For more details, you can visit their page   here (https://web.facebook.com/TimeOutCafeAndRestaurant/)

White Bird Cafe
White Bird Cafe is another must-visit café in Petra. It offers a variety of beverages and light meals, perfect for a quick break. You   can   find   more   about   them   here (https://web.facebook.com/Whitebirdcafe2).

Orient Café
Orient Cafe is known for its warm hospitality and delicious food. It's a great place to experience the local culture while enjoying a cup of coffee.

Chiffchaff Cafe
Chiffchaff Cafe is a charming café that offers a variety of food and drinks. It's a great place to unwind and enjoy the local atmosphere. Check out their page here (https://web.facebook.com/chiffchaffcafe/)

4.5   Markets in Jordan

4.5.1   Markets and Street Food Spots in Amman

Hashem Restaurant Downtown
This is a fixture on the city's food scene, and it is known for serving the best fuul. Fuul is a traditional Middle Eastern dish made from fava beans and it's a must-try when you're in Amman. More Info at https://hashemrestaurants.com/en/

Soak Jara
Although it only opens on Fridays, Soak Jara is one of the best markets in Amman showcasing the handmade work of local artisans. It's located next to Rainbow Street.

Friday Market

The Friday Market is another popular spot in Amman. It's a great place to find a variety of items, from clothes to household goods.

Falafel Al-Quds

Located on Rainbow Street, Falafel Al-Quds serves only falafel sandwiches. It's a popular spot for both locals and tourists.

When visiting these markets, it's important to remember that bargaining is a common practice. Don't be afraid to negotiate the price, especially at the Friday Market. Also, try to visit the markets early in the day when they're less crowded.

4.5.2 Markets in Aqaba

Fish Market

The Fish Market in Aqaba is a must-visit for seafood lovers. Located near the port, this bustling market is where local fishermen sell their daily catch. You'll find a wide variety of fresh seafood, including fish, shrimp, squid, and more. The market is open early in the morning, so it's best to go early to get the freshest selection.

After purchasing, you can take your seafood to one of the nearby restaurants where they will cook it for you. Prices vary depending on the type and quantity of seafood you buy, but it's generally affordable and definitely worth the experience.

4.5.3 Markets in Petra

Town Bazaar

The Town Bazaar is a popular shopping destination in Petra. Here, you can find a variety of items ranging from local handicrafts to souvenirs. It's a great place to experience the local culture and pick up unique items.
- **Address:** 8FCH+9W7, Wadi Musa, Jordan
- **Phone:** 07 9923 2928
- **Rating:** 4.6 (based on 86 reviews)
- Google Maps Link

Souk Zara Petra

Souk Zara Petra is another excellent market to visit. It offers a wide range of products, and it's a perfect place to shop for gifts and souvenirs.

- **Address:** Souk Zara, Grand Hyatt Amman Hotel, Amman, Jordan
- **Phone:** (06) 465 1433
- **Rating:** 3.9 (based on 10 reviews)
- **Website:** Souk Zara Souvenir and Handicraft shop: https://www.facebook.com/SoukZara/

Petra Rosemary Shop & Frankincense

This shop specializes in selling rosemary and frankincense, among other items. It's a unique place to visit and offers a different shopping experience.

- **Address:** Petra Moon Hotel / Lobby area Petra /Wadi Mousa, Jordan
- **Phone:** 07 7624 0340
- **Rating:** 4.6 (based on 9 reviews)
- **Website:** Petra Rosemary Shop & Frankincense on Facebook: https://www.facebook.com/people/Petra-Rosemary/100066764336803/

As for street food, here are some options:

Petra Visitor's Center

Right outside the main entrance to Petra Archaeological Park, this area has several stalls selling falafel, shawarma, hummus and other classic Jordanian street foods. Prices are slightly inflated due to its prime tourist location, but the quality is reliably good. Grab a quick bite before or after exploring the ancient city.

Sharah Main Street

The busy main thoroughfare in Wadi Musa town has sidewalk stalls grilling kebabs, chicken shawarma wraps, turkey shawarma, and traditional bedouin breads like shrak. The competition keeps quality high and prices very affordable for both locals and visitors.

Al-Wadi Restaurant
Near the Petra Marriott Hotel, this local favorite serves outstanding cheap eats like falafel sandwiches, fresh juices and turkish coffee in an open-air courtyard. The casual setting and friendly service make it a great stop. Cash only.

The Basin Restaurant
Set atop a hill near the Crowne Plaza Hotel, this landmark restaurant has stunning views of Petra. Beyond the upscale dining room, they also operate a small street food window outside serving bargains like felafel, hummus and mutabbal (eggplant dip).

Bedouin Shops near Little Petra
Stop for a break at one of the roadside Bedouin-run souvenir shops along the road near Little Petra. Sip tea and snacks like labneh (strained yogurt) with olive oil, local herbs and flatbread baked over an open fire.

Meat On Fire Restaurant
This restaurant is known for its delicious food. It's a great place to try local dishes and enjoy the vibrant atmosphere of Petra.
- **Address:** Wadi Musa, Jordan
- **Phone:** 07 7913 7837
- **Rating:** 4.9 (based on 1021 reviews)
- Google Maps Link

Yummy Bite
Yummy Bite is another excellent place to enjoy street food in Petra. They offer a variety of dishes that are sure to satisfy your taste buds.
- **Address:** Main Street‹ Wadi Musa, Jordan
- **Phone:** 07 7765 7064
- **Rating:** 4.5 (based on 116 reviews)
- Google Maps Link

Mr. Falafel - Petra
Mr. Falafel is a popular spot for locals and tourists alike. They serve delicious falafel and other Middle Eastern dishes.

- **Address:** Tourist Street Petra - wadi mousa, وادي موسى 71810, Jordan
- **Phone:** 07 9018 4517
- **Rating:** 4.8 (based on 716 reviews)
- **Website:** Mr. Falafel - Petra (https://mr-falafel-petra.business.site/)

5 Shopping in Jordan

5.1 Shopping in Amman

Here are some of the best places for shopping in Amman, Jordan:

City Mall
City Mall is one of the top shopping destinations in Amman. It offers a wide range of international and local brands, making it a great place for fashion, electronics, and more. You can also find a variety of dining options here.

Taj Lifestyle Center
Taj Mall is one of the biggest shopping malls in Amman. It consists of around 200 outlets and rooftop restaurants, offering a diverse shopping and dining experience.

Mecca Mall
Mecca Mall is another large shopping center in Amman. It offers a variety of shops and entertainment options, including a cinema and a food court.

The Galleria Mall
The Galleria Mall is a modern shopping destination in Amman. It offers a mix of high-end and affordable brands, as well as a variety of dining options.

Abdali Mall
Abdali Mall is a shopping and entertainment complex located in the new downtown area of Abdali in Amman. It offers a wide range of shops, restaurants, and entertainment options.

Baraka Mall
Baraka Mall is a shopping center located in the Sweifieh area of Amman. It offers a variety of shops, restaurants, and a cinema.

Local Souks
If you're searching for authentic Jordanian keepsakes and artisan products, there is no better place to explore than the local souks (markets). Here you can find handmade crafts, traditional clothing, spices, and more.

5.2   Shopping in Aqaba

Here are some of the best places for shopping in Aqaba, Jordan:

Aqaba City Center Shopping Mall
This is the largest mall in the city, offering a wide variety of stores for all your shopping needs. From fashion to electronics, you can find almost everything here. It's a great place to spend a day shopping and dining.

Aqaba Gateway
This is another popular shopping destination in Aqaba. It offers a variety of stores and is a great place to find unique items.

Shweikh Mall
Known as one of the best malls in Aqaba, Shweikh Mall includes a large group of various stores, which includes clothes, accessories, children's clothing, and more.

Dream Mall
This mall offers a variety of stores for shopping. It's a great place to find fashion items and more.

The Y Store
This store is known for its unique items and is a great place to find something special.

Souk by the Sea
This is a traditional market where you can find a variety of local products. It's a great place to experience the local culture and find unique souvenirs.

Please note that the average cost per item can vary greatly depending on what you're looking to buy. It's always a good idea to compare prices at different stores to ensure you're getting the best deal. Enjoy your shopping in Aqaba!

5.3   Shopping in Petra

Below are some of the best places to shop in Petra,.

Town Bazaar
The Town Bazaar is a popular shopping destination in Petra. Here, you can find a variety of items, from traditional Jordanian crafts to modern souvenirs. It's a great place to browse and soak up the local atmosphere.

Souk Zara Petra
Souk Zara Petra is another must-visit shopping destination. This market offers a wide range of items, including traditional Jordanian clothing, perfumes, and creams.

Petra Rosemary Shop & Frankincense
This shop specializes in natural products like rosemary and frankincense. It's a great place to buy unique, locally made gifts.

Mosa Spring Gift Shop
Mosa Spring Gift Shop is known for its wide selection of gifts and souvenirs. Whether you're looking for ceramics, mosaic art, or other traditional Jordanian items, you're likely to find it here.

Nabataean Ladies Cooperative
The Nabataean Ladies Cooperative is a unique shopping destination in Petra. Here, you can buy products directly from local artisans, supporting the local community in the process.

Remember, when shopping in Petra, it's common to haggle over prices. Don't be shy about negotiating - it's part of the local culture!

6   Top Attractions in Amman

Here are some key attractions in Amman.

6.1   The Amman Citadel

The Amman Citadel, known in Arabic as Jabal Al-Qal'a, is an archaeological site located in the heart of downtown Amman, the capital of Jordan. This L-shaped hill is one of the seven hills (jabals) that originally made up Amman.

The Citadel has a long history of occupation by many great civilizations, with evidence of inhabitance dating back to the Neolithic period. The hill was fortified during the Bronze Age (1800 BCE) and became the capital of the Kingdom of Ammon sometime after 1200 BCE.

It later came under the control of various empires such as the Neo-Assyrian Empire, Neo-Babylonian Empire, the Ptolemies, the Seleucids, Romans, Byzantines, and the Umayyads. Despite periods of decline, the Citadel of Amman is considered to be among the world's oldest continuously inhabited places.

Main Structures
The major remains at the site are from the Roman, Byzantine, and Umayyad periods. The main structures include:
- o   The Roman Temple of Hercules
- o   The Umayyad Palace and mosque
- o   The Byzantine church
- o   The Ayyubid watchtower

The Temple of Hercules dates back to the Roman period in the 2nd
century CE. During the Umayyad period (AD 661–750), a palace structure, known in Arabic as al-Qasr, was built at the Citadel. The palace draws on Byzantine architectural patterns and was probably used as an administrative building or the residence of an Umayyad official.

Tourism

94

The Amman Citadel is a popular tourist destination. Starting in 1995–96, the Ministry of Tourism and Antiquities of Jordan, in partnership with USAID, began a project to conserve and restore this site to benefit tourists and the local community. The Citadel is also the site of the Jordan Archaeological Museum, which houses a collection of artifacts from the Citadel and other Jordanian historic sites.

Location and How to Get There

The Citadel is located in the center of downtown Amman. It is easily accessible by taxi or car from any part of the city. If you're staying in the downtown area, it's also possible to walk to the Citadel.

Location:
- The Citadel is located on Jabal al-Qala'a, a prominent hill in downtown Amman, the capital of Jordan.
- It sits at the highest point in Amman at about 850 m (2,790 ft) above sea level.
- The Citadel complex overlooks the older downtown area of Amman, providing excellent views of the cityscape.

Arriving by Taxi:
- Taxis can directly drive you up the winding road to the Citadel entrance.
- Be sure to agree on a price before getting in the taxi. It should be 2-3 JOD from downtown.
- Ask the driver to wait if you want a ride back down to downtown. Alternatively, taxis are also available at the bottom of the hill.

Arriving by Bus:
- Take any minibus going west along Queen Rania Street to the "Citadel, Jordan Museum" stop.
- Get off across from the Jordan Museum, then walk up the road 600m to reach the Citadel entrance.
- Minibuses #25 and #26 also stop right at the bottom of the path leading up to the Citadel.

On Foot:
- If staying downtown, the Citadel is walkable in about 20-30 minutes from the King Hussein Mosque area.

- Follow King Hussein St west, then keep left on Queen Rania St until reaching the uphill road to the Citadel.

Opening Times

The Amman Citadel is open from Saturday to Thursday from 8:00 AM to 7:00 PM and on Friday from 10:00 AM to 4:00 PM. It's recommended to check the opening times before your visit as they may vary during different seasons or due to special events.

Tips for Visiting

- Allow at least 2-3 hours to explore the Citadel - it's a sprawling site with the Temple of Hercules, Byzantine church, museum, and more. Go early in the morning or late afternoon to avoid crowds.
- Purchase a combined ticket to see the Citadel, the Jordan Archaeological Museum, and the Jordan Folklore Museum for the best value.
- Wear good walking shoes and bring water - the Citadel sits on a high hill and involves steep climbs. There is minimal shade.
- Have small bills and coins ready to pay for the optional extras like binoculars to enjoy the panoramic views over downtown Amman.
- Visit the Temple of Hercules first, then weave your way through the ruins down to the museum and the Umayyad Palace. Follow signs and maps provided.
- For context, rent one of the audio guides or hire a guided tour to learn about the layers of history across Greek, Roman, Byzantine, and Umayyad periods.
- Refill your water bottle for free in the museum and use the clean bathrooms there too before hiking back up the hill.
- If visiting in summer, go very early in the morning or late afternoon to avoid the worst heat at midday. There is minimal shade at the Citadel complex.
- Dress modestly in respect of the religious history of the site - cover knees and shoulders when visiting the Byzantine church ruins and mosque.

6.2   Roman Theater

The Roman Theater is a remarkable landmark in the city of Amman, Jordan. This ancient structure dates back to the Roman period when Amman was known as Philadelphia. The theater was built between 138 and 161 CE, during the reign of the Roman Emperor Antoninus Pius. It is a testament to Roman architectural prowess and is one of the most well-preserved structures of its kind in the world.

The theater is located on the Hashemite Plaza, in the heart of the old city of Amman. It can accommodate around 6,000 spectators and is still used today for performances and events, making it a living piece of history. The theater's design takes advantage of the hillside it was built into, and its impressive acoustics allow performers to be heard throughout the venue without the need for amplification.

Visitors can reach the Roman Theater by taxi or on foot if they are staying in downtown Amman. It's a popular tourist destination, so it's well-known among local taxi drivers. The theater is open from 8:00 AM to 4:00 PM in the winter and until 7:00 PM in the summer.

When visiting the Roman Theater, it's recommended to wear comfortable shoes as there are many steps to climb. Also, don't forget to bring a hat and sunscreen during the summer months as the open-air theater can get quite hot under the sun.
For more information, you can visit the official website of Jordan's tourism board.

Interesting Fact
The Roman Theater also houses two small museums – the Jordan Folklore Museum and the Museum of Popular Traditions. These museums showcase traditional Jordanian costumes, jewelry, and other artifacts, offering visitors a glimpse into the country's rich cultural heritage.

Tips for Visiting
- The theater is located downtown near the Hashemite Plaza, Al-Husseini Mosque, and Amman Souk. It's easily reachable by taxi or walking from central hotels.
- Plan to arrive early in the morning or late afternoon to avoid the hot midday sun, as well as large tour groups that often fill the site.
- Wear good walking shoes as you'll climb a lot of uneven stone steps. Bring water too, as there is minimal shade.

- Purchase a joint ticket to also visit the nearby Folklore Museum for a small additional fee. It provides great context on Jordanian culture.
- Walk all the way down to the base of the theater for the best views looking up at the immense stone tiers rising above you.
- Climb up through the tunnels and interior corridors to emerge onto the upper seating area. Soak in the amazing acoustics.
- Spend time wandering the restored columns and hallways underneath the seating to appreciate the intricate Roman engineering.
- Attend a musical event or theatrical performance in the evening to see the theater come alive as intended in Roman times.
- Dress modestly and be respectful when photographing local visitors, especially during times of prayer and holidays.

6.3 Royal Automobile Museum

The Royal Automobile Museum in Amman is a fascinating destination that showcases the history of Jordan from a unique perspective. Unfortunately, the official website for the museum seems to be temporarily down, so I couldn't retrieve the most current information directly from the source. However, I can provide some general information based on my training data up until September 2021.

The museum was established in 2003 by King Abdullah II in memory of his father, the late King Hussein. The museum houses a rare collection of Jordan's vehicles ranging from Hussein bin Ali's Rolls Royce Silver Ghost, to modern sports cars. These cars don't just tell the story of the royal family, but also the history of the country itself.

The museum is located in the King Hussein Park in Amman, a large and popular recreational area. It's easily accessible by car or taxi from the city center. As for the opening times, it's always best to check the most current information online or contact the museum directly, as these can change. However, as of my last update, the museum was open from 10:00 AM to 7:00 PM during the summer (April to September), and from 10:00 AM to 5:00 PM during the winter (October to March).

Visitors often praise the museum for its well-maintained and diverse collection of cars, as well as its informative displays. It's definitely a must-visit for car enthusiasts, but also for anyone interested in the history of Jordan.

6.4   King Abdullah I Mosque

The King Abdullah I Mosque is a significant landmark in Amman, Jordan. The mosque was built between 1982 and 1989 as a memorial by the late King Hussein to his grandfather, King Abdullah I, the first King of Jordan. The mosque is capped by a magnificent blue mosaic dome and can accommodate up to 7,000 worshippers, with a further 3,000 in the courtyard area.

The mosque is open to non-Muslim visitors, offering a chance to understand the Muslim culture and religion. It's a must-visit for anyone interested in architecture, history, or religion. The mosque's blue dome is a distinctive feature of Amman's skyline and can be seen from various points in the city.

The mosque is considered to be one of the most impressive modern structures in Jordan. Its design is a blend of traditional Islamic architecture with Jordanian influences, resulting in a unique and beautiful building.

Location and Opening Times

The King Abdullah I Mosque is located in the heart of Amman. It's easily accessible by public transport or taxi. As for the opening times, it's recommended to check the latest information online or at your hotel as they can vary, especially during religious holidays.

Visiting Tips

- The mosque is located on a hilltop in downtown Amman, very close to the Citadel and Roman Amphitheater.
- Visit in the morning before noon prayers or in the late afternoon to avoid crowds and experience the serene atmosphere.
- Dress conservatively - women must cover their hair, arms, and legs. Loose, modest clothing that covers knees and shoulders is required for both genders.
- Be respectful by not raising your voice or taking photos inside the prayer hall when people are praying. Taking photos of the impressive exterior and dome is fine.
- Take time to appreciate the beautiful details of the mosque's architecture and décor - notice the intricate mosaic tilework and carved wood ceilings.
- Sit for a few quiet moments in the tranquil courtyard or gardens and take in the hilltop views of Amman.
- Visitors are welcome to observe prayers but non-Muslims cannot participate directly in rituals. Watch respectfully from the back.
- Remove your shoes before entering carpeted prayer areas. Footwear racks are provided.
- Free guided tours may be available to learn more about Islamic history and culture. Inquire at the entrance.

6.5 The Jordan Museum

The Jordan Museum, located in the Ras Al-Ein district of Amman, is the largest museum in Jordan and hosts the country's most important archaeological findings. Established in 2014, the museum spans over 10,000 square meters and is situated near the Greater Amman Municipality headquarters. It's only a 20-minute walk from major archaeological sites in Amman such as the Roman theater, Nymphaeum, Amman Citadel, and The Hashemite Plaza.

The museum's collections are arranged in chronological order and feature artifacts from various prehistoric archaeological sites in Jordan. Two of its main permanent exhibitions are the Dead Sea Scrolls, including the Copper Scroll, and the 9000-year-old 'Ain Ghazal statues, which are among the oldest human statues ever made. The museum also includes lecture halls, outdoor exhibitions, a library, a conservation centre, and an area for children's activities.

The Jordan Museum was established by a committee headed by Queen Rania, which became the only museum in Jordan to implement modern artifact-preserving technologies. The museum was developed to meet international standards, with construction starting in 2009 and the official opening in 2014.

The museum's collection includes animal bones dating back to 1.5 million years, 9000-year-old 'Ain Ghazal lime plaster statues, part of the Dead Sea Scrolls, including the Copper Scroll, and a reproduction of the Mesha Stele. The human statues found at 'Ain Ghazal constitute one of the world's oldest human statues ever made by human civilization dating back to 7000 BC. 'Ain Ghazal is a major Neolithic village in Amman that was discovered in 1981.

The Dead Sea Copper Scroll was found near Khirbet Qumran, which is an inventory of hidden gold and silver in specie, presumably taken from the Temple in Jerusalem in circa 68 CE. It is written in a Mishnaic-style of Hebrew. The Mesha Stele is a large black basalt stone that was erected in Moab and was inscribed by Moabite king Mesha, in which he lauds himself for the building projects that he initiated in Moab (modern day Al-Karak) and commemorates his glory and victory against the Israelites. The stele constitutes one of the most important direct accounts of biblical history.

Tips for Visiting

- The museum is easily accessible via the Amman Bus Rapid Transit line 99. The museum is also family-friendly with a dedicated area for children's activities.
- Purchase tickets in advance online or at the museum ticket office to avoid long queues, especially during peak season.
- Give yourself at least 2-3 hours to properly explore the museum's exhibits spanning Jordanian history and culture.
- Use the free coat and bag check near the entrance so you don't have to carry items throughout the galleries.
- Pick up a free map at the entrance to navigate the two floors of exhibits. Move chronologically from early history up through modern times.
- Don't miss the open-air section with ancient artifacts like the Ain Ghazal Statues and the Mesha Stele.
- The museum cafe offers respite with good coffee, snacks, and views of Amman Citadel.
- Photography is permitted but no flash or tripods. Be respectful of other visitors when taking photos.
- If visiting with kids, utilize the Children's Museum with interactive activities tailored for young ages.
- Docents are on hand throughout exhibits to answer questions and provide extra details. Don't hesitate to ask!

Rainbow Street, originally named Abu Bakr al Siddiq street, is a vibrant public space located in the historic area of Jabal Amman, near the center of downtown Amman, Jordan. The street runs east from the First Circle to Mango Street, and is a hub of activity with several attractions ranging from rooftop restaurants to pubs.

The street is home to numerous companies and shops, including the Wild Jordan Center. It also hosts important sites from modern Jordanian history, such as the al-Mufti House, the residence of King Talal (Teta Alice's House), and the home of former military commander and Prime Minister Zaid ibn Shaker. Souk Jara, a popular market, is located near the street.

Location and How to Get There
Rainbow Street is situated in the historic area of Jabal Amman, near the center of downtown Amman. It runs east from the First Circle to Mango Street. It's easily accessible by taxi or public transportation from various parts of the city.

Opening Times

Rainbow Street is a public street and is open 24/7. However, the opening times of the various shops, restaurants, and attractions along the street may vary.

Tips for Visiting

- Rainbow Street is a bustling area with a lot to offer. It's recommended to take a leisurely stroll along the street to fully enjoy the atmosphere and explore the various shops and eateries. Don't forget to check out the Wild Jordan Center and the historic sites along the street.
- Rainbow Street is located in the Jebel Amman neighborhood, around 15-20 minutes by taxi from downtown. Get dropped off at the Rainbow intersection.
- Go in the early evening around 5-7pm when the street really comes alive and the temperatures cool down. Many cafes stay open late.
- The street is very walkable. Wander slowly, popping into any art galleries, shops, or cafes that catch your eye.
- Make time to browse famous books shop al-Hikma, and stop for coffee at local hangouts like Rumi or Duinde.
- For dinner, try popular restaurants like Sufra, Levant, or Wild Jordan (located just off Rainbow Street). Make reservations in peak season.
- The area is very safe to explore solo or in groups. You'll see plenty of other tourists mixing with locals.
- Dress is casual. Jordanians here are used to seeing foreigners. But be respectful and avoid revealing clothing.
- Visit on a Friday morning to combine your outing with the bustling Souk Jara market just downhill from Rainbow Street.
- Consider booking one of the guided food or walking tours to learn more about the area's culture and history from a local guide.

Interesting Fact

Rainbow Street is not just a hub for shopping and dining, but it's also a place steeped in history. It's home to important sites from modern Jordanian history, including the al-Mufti House, the residence of King Talal (Teta Alice's House), and the home of former military commander and Prime Minister Zaid ibn Shaker.

Darat al Funun, located in Amman, is a home for the arts and artists from the Arab world. It was founded in 1988 by Suha Shoman and has become a meeting place for artists and a hub for artistic practices. The cultural haven is dedicated to contemporary art and features a series of galleries and outdoor spaces displaying its collections and special exhibitions with a focus on contemporary artists of the Arab world.

The main building features an excellent art gallery, providing visitors with an immersive experience into the world of contemporary Arab art. The institution is situated on the hillside to the north of the downtown area, making it a convenient location for tourists and locals alike.

Visiting hours are from 10 AM to 7 PM from Saturday to Thursday. For more information, you can visit their official website here.

When planning your visit, it's recommended to check their current exhibitions and events to make the most of your experience. Also, don't forget to respect the art and the space, and enjoy the creativity and talent on display.

7   Top Attractions in Petra

7.1   Al-Khazneh (The Treasury)

Al-Khazneh, also known as The Treasury, is one of the most elaborate temples in the ancient Arab Nabatean Kingdom city of Petra. This stunning piece of architecture is carved out of a sandstone rock face and has classical Greek-influenced architecture. It has been designated as a UNESCO World Heritage Site and is a symbol of Jordan, as well as its most-visited tourist attraction.

The Treasury was first built in the 1st century AD as a mausoleum and crypt. The name "Treasury" comes from the legend that bandits or pirates hid their loot in a stone urn high on the second level. It was believed to be filled with treasures, but the urn is solid sandstone, and the name is now used more widely for the entire building.

The Treasury is located at the end of Petra's Siq, a narrow gorge winding through towering sandstone cliffs. The first glimpse of the Treasury from the Siq is a defining moment and a symbol of Jordan's tourist industry.

The site is open from 6 AM to 6 PM in the summer and 6 AM to 4 PM in the winter. The entrance fee to Petra includes the visit to the Treasury. It's recommended to visit early in the morning or late in the afternoon when the crowds are smaller.

Please note that while the facade of the Treasury is accessible to tourists, the interior is not open to the public. The best way to get to Petra is by car or by joining a tour from Amman or Aqaba.

7.2   Ad-Deir (The Monastery)

Ad-Deir, also known as The Monastery, is one of the most iconic structures in Petra. It's an impressive example of the Nabatean architecture, carved directly into the sandstone cliff face.

The Monastery gets its name from the crosses inscribed inside, suggesting it was used as a Christian church during the Byzantine era. However, it was initially built as a Nabatean tomb or temple.

The facade of Ad-Deir is stunning and measures approximately 50 meters wide and 45 meters high, making it one of the largest structures in Petra. The architectural design is similar to Al-Khazneh (The Treasury), but it's much larger and less intricate.

To reach Ad-Deir, visitors must climb a path of about 800 steps that wind through the mountains of Petra. The journey can be quite strenuous, but the breathtaking views at the top are well worth the effort.

Once at the top, visitors can enter the monument's single, vast chamber and admire the two levels of the facade, crowned by a magnificent urn.

Please note that the opening times can vary, and it's always a good idea to check the official Petra visitor's site or contact your tour guide for the most accurate information.

Remember to bring plenty of water, wear comfortable shoes, and take your time to enjoy the stunning scenery along the way to Ad-Deir.

7.3   Siq

The Siq is the main entrance to the ancient city of Petra in southern Jordan. The dim, narrow gorge (in some points no more than 3 meters wide) winds its way approximately 1.2 kilometers and ends at Petra's most elaborate ruin, Al Khazneh (the Treasury).

A natural geological feature formed from a deep split in the sandstone rocks, the Siq is a stunning place to walk through due to its high walls that impressively narrow down before revealing the first glimpse of the Treasury.

The Siq has walls that reach up to 200 meters in height and it was used as the grand caravan entrance into Petra. Along both walls of the Siq are a number of votive niches containing baetyli, which suggest that the Siq was sacred to the Nabatean people.

In terms of visiting, the Siq is open during the operating hours of the Petra Archaeological Park, which typically opens from 6 AM to 6 PM in the summer and 6 AM to 4 PM in the winter. However, these times can change, so it's recommended to check the official website or contact the park directly for the most accurate information.

Please note that it's a bit of a walk to get from the visitor center to the Siq and then onto the Treasury, so be sure to wear comfortable shoes, bring water, and prepare for the weather.

7.4   Royal Tombs

The Royal Tombs are one of the most significant attractions in Petra. They are a series of impressive tombs carved into the rock face of the city's western cliffs. The name "Royal Tombs" is a misnomer as it's not confirmed that they were indeed for royalty, but the grandeur of these tombs implies significant importance.

The Royal Tombs consist of the Urn Tomb, the Silk Tomb, the Corinthian Tomb, and the Palace Tomb. Each of these tombs is unique in its architectural style and size. The Urn Tomb is particularly notable for its large courtyard and intricately carved facade.

Visitors can reach the Royal Tombs by walking from the city center. They are located after the Street of Facades, another notable site in Petra. The tombs are usually open during the daylight hours, but it's always a good idea to check the official Petra visitor site for the most accurate and up-to-date information.

As for tips, it's recommended to wear comfortable shoes as there's a lot of walking and climbing involved. Also, don't forget to bring water and sun protection as Petra can get quite hot, especially in the summer.

Please be aware that the information might vary, and it's always a good idea to check the most recent updates before your visit.

7.5 Petra Theater

The Petra Theater is an impressive monument carved out of a rock face. It was built by the Nabataeans in the 1st century AD and later enlarged by the Romans. The theater has the capacity to seat about 4,000 spectators. It's a testament to the architectural prowess of the Nabataeans and offers a glimpse into the entertainment culture of the time.

The theater is located near the center of the ancient city, not far from the famous Treasury. It's easily accessible along the main path through Petra.

As for visiting hours, Petra archaeological park is generally open from 6:00 AM to 6:00 PM in the summer and 6:00 AM to 4:00 PM in the winter. However, it's always a good idea to check the official website or contact the park directly for the most up-to-date information.

Please note that the theater, like many of the structures in Petra, is an ancient monument. Visitors are asked to respect the site and refrain from climbing on the structures to prevent damage.

The Colonnaded Street is one of the significant archaeological features in Petra. It's a remnant of the city's Roman past, dating back to around the 2nd century AD. This was once the city's main commercial street, lined with shops and bustling with trade.

The street is paved and flanked by columns on both sides, hence the name "Colonnaded Street". It leads from the city center towards Qasr al-Bint, one of the few free-standing buildings in Petra that has remained intact. While the columns and the paved road are the most visible remnants, there were also once numerous buildings along this street, including markets and public spaces. Today, you can still see the foundations and parts of the walls of these structures.

Visiting the Colonnaded Street gives you a glimpse into the daily life of ancient Petra, where people would have walked, shopped, and conducted business. It's a testament to the city's past grandeur and its importance as a trading hub.

Please note that the opening times of Petra archaeological park are usually from 6:00 AM to 6:00 PM in the summer and 6:00 AM to 4:00 PM in the winter. However, it's always a good idea to check the official website or contact the park directly for the most accurate and up-to-date information.

Remember to wear comfortable shoes and bring water, as exploring Petra involves a lot of walking. Also, hiring a local guide can enrich your experience as they can provide more detailed historical context and show you less-known spots.

7.7 High Place of Sacrifice

The High Place of Sacrifice, also known as Al-Madbah, is one of the most intriguing sites in Petra. It is a religious altar that was used for sacrificial ceremonies. The site is located at the summit of Jebel Madbah, which is a mountain that overlooks the ancient city of Petra.
The High Place of Sacrifice is accessible via a steep and rocky path that starts near the Street of Facades. The climb to the top can be quite challenging, but it's worth it for the panoramic views of Petra and the surrounding landscape.

At the top, you'll find two obelisks carved out of the rock, which are believed to represent the Nabatean gods Dushara and Al-Uzza. There's also a platform with a ceremonial altar, where animal sacrifices were believed to have been conducted.

The site is typically open during daylight hours, but it's always a good idea to check with local authorities or your tour guide for the most current information. Also, remember to bring water and sun protection, as the climb can be hot and there's little shade.

As for the exact location and opening times, I recommend checking with the local tourist information center or your hotel concierge when you arrive in Petra. They will have the most up-to-date information.

Please note that while visiting historical and archaeological sites, it's important to respect the rules and guidelines to help preserve these precious sites for future generations.

Remember, the journey to the High Place of Sacrifice can be quite strenuous, so it's recommended for those in good physical condition. But the view from the top is truly spectacular and offers a unique perspective on the ancient city of Petra.

7.8   Little Petra (Siq al-Barid)

Little Petra, also known as Siq al-Barid, is a smaller but equally fascinating archaeological site located north of Petra. It is believed to have been an important suburb of Petra, the capital of the Nabatean Arabs, and it is thought to have served as a stopover point for the caravans that travelled along the Silk Road.

The site is home to several notable structures, including tombs, temples, and dining halls, many of which feature the same intricate rock-cut architecture as the buildings in Petra. One of the highlights of Little Petra is the Painted House, a dining hall decorated with Hellenistic-style frescoes, which are a rare example of Nabatean figurative painting.

Little Petra is located about 9 km north of Petra, and it can be reached by car or taxi from the city of Wadi Musa. The site is open from sunrise to sunset, and there is no entrance fee. However, it's worth noting that the site is less developed than Petra, with fewer facilities and services available.

Visiting Little Petra offers a chance to experience the wonder of Nabatean architecture and history in a quieter, less crowded setting. It's a must-visit for anyone interested in archaeology and the ancient world.

8 Top Attractions in Jerash

8.1 Jerash Ruins

Jerash is a city in Jordan, located 48 kilometers north of the capital Amman. It is known for the ruins of the ancient city of Gerasa, also referred to as Antioch on the Golden River.

Historical Background

Ancient Jerash was originally inhabited by the Greeks and later conquered by the Romans. During the Roman period, it was one of the ten wealthy, self-governing cities of the Decapolis and was famous for its arts and culture. The city flourished until the mid-eighth century CE when the 749 Galilee earthquake destroyed large parts of it. The Crusaders described Jerash as uninhabited, and it remained abandoned until its rediscovery in the early 19th century.

Architectural Highlights

The ruins of Jerash include a number of notable structures. The Corinthium column, Hadrian's Arch, a hippodrome, two immense temples dedicated to Zeus and Artemis, the nearly unique oval Forum, which is surrounded by a fine colonnade, a long colonnaded street, two theatres, two baths, a scattering of small temples, and an almost complete circuit of city walls. Most of these monuments were built by donations of the city's wealthy citizens.

Visiting Jerash

When visiting Jerash, it's recommended to wear comfortable shoes as you'll be walking a lot. The site is quite large and there's a lot to see. It's also a good idea to bring a hat and sunscreen as there's not much shade.

The site is open from 8:00 AM to 5:00 PM in the winter and from 8:00 AM to 6:00 PM in the summer. It's also open on Fridays and holidays from 10:00 AM to 6:00 PM in the summer and from 10:00 AM to 4:00 PM in the winter.

Getting There

Here is an extensive guide to getting to the ancient Roman city of Jerash from Amman, Jordan:
Jerash is located about 48 km (30 miles) north of Amman. It takes around 1 hour to reach by private car or taxi, or a bit longer by public transportation.

By Taxi:
- Easily arranged from your Amman hotel, or hail a taxi from downtown. Agree on price before departing, expect to pay 25-35 JOD ($35-50 USD) each way.
- Ask the driver to wait if you want a return ride. Clarify this and negotiate an hourly rate for waiting time.

By Private Car & Driver:
- Hiring a private car and driver for the day offers maximum flexibility for touring Jerash. Rates start around 80-100 JOD ($110-140 USD).
- Recommended if combining Jerash with other northern sights like Ajloun Castle. Your driver can customize the day's itinerary.

By Rental Car:
- Renting a car allows independence to visit Jerash at your own pace. Expect rates around 30-60 JOD ($42-85) per day.
- Use offline maps/GPS as signage en route is limited. Exit Amman north on Highway 15 toward Jerash.

By Bus from Amman:

- Public buses offer the cheapest way to reach Jerash. Take bus #261 from Raghadan Station (Tabarbour) in north Amman.
- Buses depart hourly most of the day. The journey takes 90+ minutes each way depending on traffic. Schedule returns carefully.
- Tickets cost just over 1 JOD ($1.40 USD) each way. Bring small bills to pay fare on-board. Buses can get crowded.

Guided Day Tour:
- Booking a Jerash day tour from Amman includes transport and a guide. Prices range 60-100 JOD ($85-140 USD) per person.
- Popular option if you prefer not to navigate public transportation or drive yourself.

Jerash is a fascinating city with a rich history and well-preserved ruins. It's definitely worth a visit if you're in Jordan.

8.2 Ajloun Castle

Ajloun Castle, also known as Qal'at 'Ajloun, is a 12th-century Muslim castle located in northwestern Jordan. The castle is situated on a hilltop in the Mount Ajloun district, also known as Jabal 'Auf. This strategic location allowed the castle to guard three wadis that descend towards the Jordan Valley. The castle was initially built by the Ayyubids in the 12th century and later expanded by the Mamluks in the 13th century.

History
The castle's site was originally an old monastery, with the name 'Ajlun believed to be derived from a Christian monk who lived in

the area during the Byzantine period. The castle was rebuilt in 1184 by Izz al-Din Usama, a general in the army of Saladin, primarily to control the Bedouin tribes of the Jabal 'Auf and protect against Crusader incursions. The castle also protected the iron mines of Ajlun.

In the 13th century, the castle was expanded by the Mamluk governor, Aibak ibn Abdullah. However, the castle suffered significant damage during the Mongol invasions of 1260 AD. It was later restored by the Mamluk Sultan ad-Dhaher Baibars.

Tourism
Today, Ajloun Castle is a popular tourist destination. Visitors can explore many areas of the castle, including a museum exhibition showcasing artifacts from various historical periods. The castle offers a unique perspective on Jordan's rich history and cultural significance.

Location and Opening Times
Here are the opening times and schedule for visiting Ajloun Castle in Jordan:
- Ajloun Castle is open daily from 8:00am to 6:00pm during the summer season (April to September).
- In the winter from October to March, it is open from 8:00am to 4:00pm.
- The ticket office closes one hour before the stated closing time of the castle.
- Fridays and official holidays have the same opening hours. The site remains open during Ramadan.
- Occasionally parts of the castle may close on short notice for unscheduled maintenance or events. Check ahead of time.
- Tickets cost 3 JD (around $4 USD) for non-students. Children under 12 enter for 1 JD.
- Tickets can be purchased at the main entrance gate upon arrival. Cash is preferred though credit cards may be accepted.
- Guided tours are not necessary, but private licensed guides can be hired on-site for an additional fee. Inquire at the ticket window.
- English information plaques are available throughout the castle complex providing good background on the architecture and history.

- Audio guides are also available to rent for a small fee and add deeper context.

Getting to Ajloun Castle early in the day allows sufficient time to explore the sprawling hilltop ruins and take in the views of the countryside. Keep the operating hours in mind when visiting as part of your Jordan itinerary.

Getting There
Ajloun is approximately 73 kilometers north of Amman, Jordan's capital. The journey can be made by car or by public transport. There are regular buses from Amman's North Bus Station to Ajloun. Once in Ajloun, the castle is a short taxi ride or a moderate uphill walk from the town center. More details:

By Bus from Amman:
- Public buses are the cheapest way to reach Ajloun Castle. Take bus #412 from Tabarbour Bus Station (North Station) in Amman.
- Buses depart hourly and take around 2 hours to reach Ajloun depending on traffic. Schedule your return bus carefully.
- Tickets cost around 2 JD ($2.80 USD) each way. Pay cash on board. Buses can be crowded.
- Get off in downtown Ajloun. The castle is around 2.5 km uphill from the bus stop. Take a taxi or walk the rest of the way.

By Taxi/Car Service from Amman:
- Hiring a taxi or car service allows door-to-door transport directly to the castle entrance.
- The drive takes around 90 minutes from Amman depending on traffic.
- Agree on a fixed price before departing. Expect to pay around 60-80 JD ($85-115 USD) for a private roundtrip transfer.

By Rental Car:
- Renting a car gives flexibility to visit Ajloun Castle and other northern Jordan sights.

- Take Highway 15 out of Amman, then follow signs to Ajloun via Highway 30. Total drive is around 90 km (56 miles).
- Use offline maps or GPS as road signage is limited. There is parking at the castle site.

Guided Day Tour:
- Many reputable tour companies offer full-day trips to Ajloun Castle from Amman by AC coach.
- Tours include hotel pickup/drop-off, transportation, English guide, some include lunch.
- Prices range 60-120 JD ($85-170 USD) per person depending on group size and inclusions.

Tips for Visiting
- Give yourself at least 2 hours to fully explore the large castle grounds and ruins at a relaxed pace. Go early to beat the crowds.
- Wear sturdy shoes as you'll be climbing stone steps and walking over uneven ruined surfaces. Bring a hat and water too.
- Pick up a free map at the entrance to help navigate the various sections like the towers, kitchens, cisterns, and courtyard.
- Take time to enjoy the information panels and signage explaining each area's history and original use during medieval times.
- Climb the steep steps up to the upper towers for stunning panoramic views over the countryside. This was a key military vantage point.
- Search the ground around the citadel walls and lower courtyard to find ancient coins and shards of pottery left behind over centuries.
- The nearby Islamic-era Ajloun Castle Museum is also worth a quick visit to see local artifacts.
- Budget extra time to stop into the helpful visitor's center to watch their informative video detailing the castle's expansive history.
- Visit early or late in the day to have the impressive hilltop ruins and surrounds to yourself before tourist buses arrive.

8.3 South Theatre

The South Theatre is a well-preserved Roman theater that could seat more than 3000 spectators. It was built during the reign of Emperor Domitian, between 90-92 AD.

8.4 Oval Plaza

The Oval Plaza, also known as the Forum, is a large public square in Jerash. It is surrounded by a broad sidewalk and a colonnade of 1st-century Ionic columns.

However, the Oval Plaza, also known as the Oval Forum, is one of the most notable structures in the ancient city of Jerash. It's a large and wide public space that was used for a variety of public and social activities. The plaza is unique due to its oval shape, which is unusual for Roman architecture typically known for its straight lines and angles.

The Oval Plaza is surrounded by a broad sidewalk and a colonnade of 1st-century Ionic columns. There are two altars in the middle, and a fountain was added in the 7th century AD. This plaza is a great place to sit and soak up the atmosphere of this amazing archaeological site.
As for the location, the Oval Plaza is located within the archaeological site of Jerash, and it's one of the first structures you'll see after entering through the Hadrian's Arch.

The site of Jerash is typically open from early morning until the evening, but the timings can change depending on the season and local holidays. It's recommended to check the official opening times before planning your visit.

Remember to wear comfortable shoes as you'll be walking on uneven ancient stones, and don't forget to bring a hat and water during the summer months as it can get quite hot.

8.5   Temple of Artemis

Overview
The Temple of Artemis is a Roman temple in the ancient city of Gerasa, modern-day Jerash, Jordan. It was dedicated to Artemis, the patron goddess of the city who was believed to protect the city. The temple was built in the middle of the 2nd century CE during the reign of the Roman Emperor Antoninus Pius.

History
The Temple of Artemis was one of the most important structures in Gerasa. The city was part of the Decapolis, a group of ten cities on the eastern frontier of the Roman Empire in Judea and Syria. The temple was built on one of the highest points and dominated the whole city. The temple was built on a podium and was surrounded by a portico. It was richly decorated with marble and

had a grand staircase. The temple was severely damaged by earthquakes in 363 CE and 749 CE.

Interesting Facts The Temple of Artemis is known for its impressive columns. Eleven of the twelve front columns are still standing and they are an impressive 15m high. The columns are unique because they sway slightly, a feature designed to withstand earthquakes.

Visiting Tips

The Temple of Artemis is located within the archaeological site of Jerash, which is one of the most popular tourist destinations in Jordan. The site is vast and there is a lot to see, so it's recommended to allow at least half a day for your visit. It's also a good idea to wear comfortable shoes as there is a lot of walking involved.

- The Temple of Artemis is part of the sprawling ruins of ancient Jerash. Devote at least 3-4 hours to see the main sites.
- The temple's foundation and scattered columns sit just south of the city's main plaza, the Oval Piazza.
- Walk among the giant fallen columns to visualize the massive scale this temple once held when intact.
- Climb the steps and look west for views of the temple ruins framed by ancient Jerash's monumental archway.
- Spend time reading the informative signs to understand details of the temple's original construction, its destruction, and ongoing archaeological work.
- Imagine the bustling religious activity, sacrifices, and commerce that once took place here to honor the goddess Artemis.
- For context, visit the Jerash Archaeological Museum first to see statues of Artemis and other artifacts found at the temple site.
- Hire an English-speaking guide to vividly narrate stories of daily life and key events at this important temple.
- Arrive early morning or late afternoon when fewer large tourist groups are present to enjoy maximum quiet and atmosphere.
- Dress appropriately in modest clothing out of respect for the long religious history of the site.

Location and How to Get There

Jerash is located 48 kilometers north of the capital Amman. It's easily accessible by car or bus from Amman. Once you arrive in Jerash, the archaeological site is well signposted.

Opening Times
The site is open from 8:00 AM to 5:00 PM in the winter and from 8:00 AM to 7:00 PM in the summer. It's recommended to arrive early to avoid the heat and the crowds.

Please note that the information might change, so it's always a good idea to check the latest information before your visit.

Overview

The Temple of Artemis is a Roman temple in the ancient city of Gerasa, modern-day Jerash, Jordan. It was dedicated to Artemis, the patron goddess of the city who was believed to protect the city. The temple was built in the middle of the 2nd century CE during the reign of the Roman Emperor Antoninus Pius.

History

The Temple of Artemis was one of the most important structures in Gerasa. The city was part of the Decapolis, a group of ten cities on the eastern frontier of the Roman Empire in Judea and Syria. The temple was built on one of the highest points and dominated the whole city. The temple was built on a podium and was surrounded by a portico. It was richly decorated with marble and had a grand staircase. The temple was severely damaged by earthquakes in 363 CE and 749 CE.

Interesting Facts

The Temple of Artemis is known for its impressive columns. Eleven of the twelve front columns are still standing and they are an impressive 15m high. The columns are unique because they sway slightly, a feature designed to withstand earthquakes.

Visiting Tips

The Temple of Artemis is located within the archaeological site of Jerash, which is one of the most popular tourist destinations in Jordan. The site is vast and there is a lot to see, so it's recommended to allow at least half a day for your visit. It's also a good idea to wear comfortable shoes as there is a lot of walking involved.

Opening Times The site is open from 8:00 AM to 5:00 PM in the winter and from 8:00 AM to 7:00 PM in the summer. It's recommended to arrive early to avoid the heat and the crowds.
Please note that the information might change, so it's always a good idea to check the latest information before your visit.

The Arch of Hadrian, also known as Hadrian's Gate, is a triumphal arch which was built to honor the visit of Roman Emperor Hadrian to Jerash in 129/130 AD. The arch was intended to become the new southern gate of the city but the expansion plans were never completed. The arch is approximately 11 meters high and is beautifully decorated with acanthus leaves and various other sculptural decorations.

9 Top Attractions for Wadi Rum

9.1 Wadi Rum Protected Area

Overview

Wadi Rum, also known as the Valley of the Moon, is a valley cut into the sandstone and granite rock in southern Jordan. It is the largest wadi in Jordan. The Wadi Rum Protected Area is a UNESCO World Heritage site that covers an expansive desert wilderness in southern Jordan. It features dramatic sandstone mountains, natural arches, prehistoric inscriptions and carvings, and narrow gorges. The area is also home to the Bedouin tribes who live in scattered camps throughout the area. The name Rum most likely comes from an Aramaic root meaning 'high' or 'elevated'. The area is now one of Jordan's important tourist destinations and attracts an increasing number of foreign tourists, particularly trekkers and climbers, but also for camel and horse safari or simply day-trippers from Aqaba or Petra. Visitors can enjoy a variety of activities such as hiking, rock climbing, camel and horse riding, and hot air ballooning.

History

Wadi Rum has been inhabited by many human cultures since prehistoric times, with many cultures–including the Nabateans–leaving their mark in the form of rock paintings, graffiti, and temples. As of 2007, several Bedouin tribes inhabit Rum and the surrounding area.

In the West, Wadi Rum may be best known for its connection with British officer T. E. Lawrence, who based his operations here during the Arab Revolt of 1917–1918. In the 1980s, one of the rock formations in Wadi Rum was named "The Seven Pillars of Wisdom" in memory of Lawrence's book penned in the aftermath of the war, though the 'Seven Pillars' referred to in the book have no connection with Rum.

Geography and Climate
Wadi Rum is situated in a desert region with a typical hot desert climate. The area is known for its stunning natural arches, towering cliffs, massive landslides, and caverns. The highest elevation in Jordan, Jebel Um Adaami, is located at the south-west of Wadi Rum.

Visiting Wadi Rum
The visitor center, car park, a museum, and some shops and tour operators are located in Wadi Rum Village, which is the starting point for tours into the desert. The village is inhabited by Bedouin tribes and is located about 37 kilometers from the town of Aqaba. Tourists can explore the area through a variety of activities such as rock-climbing, hiking, camel and horse riding, or hot air ballooning. Camping under the stars in Bedouin tents is a popular way to experience the desert environment.

Interesting Facts
Wadi Rum's beauty is not only appreciated on Earth. The area has been used as a backdrop for numerous films, especially science fiction films set on Mars, including Red Planet, The Martian, and Star Wars: Rogue One.

Please note that the opening times and specific details about visiting Wadi Rum can vary, so it's recommended to check with a reliable tour operator or the official tourism board of Jordan for the most accurate and up-to-date information.

Jabal Khazali, also known as Khazali Canyon, is a prominent peak located in the heart of the Wadi Rum Protected Area. The mountain opens up into a narrow fissure, approximately 100 meters in length, with its inner walls adorned with a variety of ancient inscriptions and petroglyphs.

The canyon is renowned for its Thamudic, Nabatean, and Islamic inscriptions, as well as petroglyphs of humans, animals, and soles of feet. These historical markings provide a fascinating glimpse into the region's past, making it a must-visit for history enthusiasts and curious travelers alike.

Jabal Khazali is not just a historical site but also a natural wonder. The canyon's unique geological features, combined with the surrounding desert landscape, create a truly breathtaking scene. It's a perfect spot for photography, hiking, and simply appreciating the beauty of nature.

When visiting, it's recommended to wear comfortable shoes suitable for walking on uneven terrain, and don't forget to bring water and sun protection. The site is accessible by vehicle, but the last part of the journey will need to be completed on foot, navigating through the narrow canyon.

As for the opening times, it's best to check with local tour operators or the visitor center at Wadi Rum, as these can vary depending on the time of year and local conditions.

9.3 Lawrence's Spring

Lawrence's Spring is a popular tourist attraction located in Wadi Rum, Ma'in Governorate, Jordan. It is named after the British officer T.E. Lawrence, better known as Lawrence of Arabia, who reportedly washed at this spring during the Arab Revolt against the Ottoman Empire in World War I.

History and Significance
The spring is steeped in history and is named after T.E. Lawrence (Lawrence of Arabia), who made Wadi Rum his base during the 1917-1918 Arab Revolt against the Ottoman Empire. It is said that Lawrence and his Arab guerillas frequently used this spring as a vital water source. The spring is mentioned in Lawrence's book "Seven Pillars of Wisdom".

Location and How to Get There
Lawrence's Spring is located in the stunning desert landscape of Wadi Rum, also known as the Valley of the Moon, in southern Jordan. It's about 60km to the east of Aqaba. To get there, you can

take a taxi or a bus from Aqaba to Wadi Rum Village. From the village, it's a short 4x4 drive or a moderate hike to the spring.

Visiting Tips

When visiting Lawrence's Spring, be prepared for a bit of a climb. The spring is located up a small cliff. The climb is not too strenuous, but it's a good idea to wear comfortable shoes. Once you reach the spring, you'll be rewarded with a small but beautiful waterfall and some of the most breathtaking views of the Wadi Rum desert.

The spring itself is quite small and may be dry depending on the time of year. However, the real attraction is the stunning natural beauty of the surrounding area. Don't forget to bring your camera!

Opening Times

Lawrence's Spring is open to visitors all year round. However, the best time to visit Wadi Rum and Lawrence's Spring is between March and May or between September and November when the weather is more moderate.

Please note that the information about opening times and how to get there might change, so it's always a good idea to check the latest information before your visit.

Interesting Facts

The area around Lawrence's Spring is home to several ancient inscriptions and carvings. Take some time to explore and you'll discover a fascinating glimpse into the area's past.

Remember, Lawrence's Spring is not just a historical site, but also an important water source in a harsh desert environment. Please respect the site and leave no trace of your visit.

Visiting Lawrence's Spring offers a unique combination of natural beauty, historical significance, and a connection to the fascinating story of Lawrence of Arabia. It's a must-see for any visitor to Wadi Rum.

The Burdah Rock Bridge is one of the most stunning natural formations in the Wadi Rum desert of Jordan. This natural arch, standing at a height of about 35 meters, is the highest in Wadi Rum and offers an exhilarating climb and breathtaking views of the desert landscape.

History and Interesting Facts
The Burdah Rock Bridge is a product of natural erosion over millions of years. The sandstone rock in the area has been shaped

by the wind and occasional rain into various forms, one of which is this magnificent bridge. The bridge is named after the mountain it is part of, Jebel Burdah.

Location and How to Get There
The Burdah Rock Bridge is located in the Wadi Rum Protected Area in southern Jordan, about 60 km to the east of Aqaba. The best way to reach Wadi Rum is by car from Aqaba or Amman. Once in Wadi Rum, you can hire a local Bedouin guide to take you to the bridge. It's recommended to use a 4x4 vehicle to navigate the desert terrain.

Visiting Tips
Visiting the Burdah Rock Bridge is not for the faint-hearted. The climb to the top is challenging and requires a certain level of fitness. However, the effort is well worth it for the stunning views from the top. It's recommended to start the climb early in the morning to avoid the heat of the day.

Make sure to bring plenty of water, sun protection, and sturdy shoes for the climb. Also, remember that you are in a protected area, so respect the environment and leave no trace.

Opening Times
The Wadi Rum Protected Area, where the Burdah Rock Bridge is located, is open 24 hours a day, seven days a week. However, it's best to visit during daylight hours for safety reasons.

The Anfashieh Inscriptions in Wadi Rum, Jordan, are a remarkable piece of history that have been preserved for over two thousand years. These petroglyphs, etched into the rosy stone, depict simple figures and camels, resembling the drawings of a child. They were created by the Thamud and Nabatean peoples, both tribes with a mysterious history.

Historical Significance
The Thamudic people are mentioned in an inscription by Sargon II, an Assyrian king of the 8th century BCE. However, Islamic traditions and the Qur'an suggest that the Thamudic people existed earlier than this. By around 600 CE, the tribe vanished, possibly due to a volcanic eruption, earthquake, or divine intervention.

The Nabatean people, best known for their construction of Petra, emerged from obscurity around the 4th century BCE. They controlled trade routes vital to the many caravans that travelled between Egypt and Syria, and maintained independence until annexation to the Romans in 106 CE. Their civilization crumbled in the 5th century after their conversion to Christianity and succession to new invading Arab tribes.

134

Visiting the Anfashieh Inscriptions

The inscriptions are of great archaeological importance, but you do not need to be a historian to appreciate them. Just gazing at the markings made two thousand years ago is enough to awe and humble any traveller, and the chance to see them is not to be missed.

The Anfashieh inscriptions are explained and detailed as part of the Petroglyph tour, they are also seasonally included in the standard 4×4 tour, and can be incorporated for guests with a specific interest. They are located on the south facing side of Jebel Anfashieh towards Jebel Um Kharg and directly across from the entrance of Rakhabat Canyon.

The GPS coordinates are 29.55591N, 35.452947E. The location is identified on the Wadi Rum tourist map showing the all major attractions.

Interesting Facts

o   The inscriptions were inscribed by trading caravans, depicting their movement through the desert.
o   They are a combination of petroglyphs from the Thamudic and Nabatean peoples, tribes dating from approximately 700 BCE and 300 BCE respectively.

10 Culture and Entertainment in Jordan

10.1 Art Galleries in Amman

Amman Panorama Art Gallery
This gallery is located opposite the Roman Theater in downtown Amman. It is highly recommended for visitors to the city.

Darat al Funun
This is a relaxed art center with a pleasant cafe, ideal for relaxing for a few hours or just to meet and chat or take a coffee. It's located in the heart of Amman.

Dar Al-Anda Art Gallery
The place is artistic, the art is beautiful, and it offers a nice view of Amman's old city. It also has a section of artistic fashion and home decoration where items are reasonably priced.

Wadi Finan Art Gallery
This is a small art gallery just off Rainbow Street. It hosts exhibitions of work by contemporary artists from around the region.

Project Positive Soulful Creations
Run by two sisters who make beautiful dresses and jackets by hand and needle. The items are unique and reasonably priced.

Orient Gallery
This gallery showcases some of the most talented artists of the region. It has a wide variety of paintings in their ongoing exhibitions and permanent collections alike.

Ola's Garden
This is a gem of a gallery of handmade jewelry, clothing, scarves, and other art items, all made by Ola herself. It's located not far from the end of Rainbow Street.

10.2 Art Galleries in Aqaba

Arts of Sham Countries Art Gallery
Located on Raghadan Street, behind the Al-Husin Bin Ali mosque, this gallery is a must-visit for art lovers. It showcases a variety of art from the Sham countries. Unfortunately, the specific types of art, opening times, and entrance fees are not mentioned in the sources. For more detailed information, you may want to visit their website or contact them directly.

Aqaba in the Eyes of Artists
This is not a specific gallery, but rather a collection of art pieces that depict the city of Aqaba. These artworks can be found in various locations around the city.

For art galleries in Amman, Jerash, and Petra, I will need to conduct further searches.

10.3 Art Galleries in Jerash

Vaulted Gallery
The Vaulted Gallery is a part of the ancient city of Jerash, which is a significant tourist attraction in Jordan. It's a great place to learn about the three main column styles: Doric, Ionic, and Corinthian. The model of the Temple of Zeus is also worth seeing.

Gerasa Collection at The Metropolitan Museum of Art
Although not located in Jerash itself, the Gerasa Collection at The Metropolitan Museum of Art features art and artifacts from Gerasa (the ancient name for Jerash). You can explore this collection online on the Metropolitan Museum of Art website.

10.4 Art Galleries in Petra

Petra Museum
The Petra Museum is a must-visit for art and history enthusiasts. The museum's Galleries 7 and 8 showcase contemporary art, archaeology, art history, architecture, and cultural heritage. You can find more information about these galleries on the universes.art website.

Petra Collection at Yale University Art Gallery

Similar to the Gerasa Collection, the Petra Collection at Yale University Art Gallery features art related to Petra. You can explore this collection online on the Yale University Art Gallery website.

10.5 Museums in Amman

The Jordan Museum
Located in Ras Al-Ein district of Amman, the Jordan Museum is the largest museum in Jordan. It houses a collection of artifacts from archaeological sites in Jordan, dating from prehistoric times to the 15th century. The museum's exhibits are arranged in chronological order and include a wide range of items, from ancient statues and coins to Islamic art and manuscripts. The museum is open from 9:00 AM to 5:00 PM from Saturday to Thursday, and from 2:00 PM to 5:30 PM on Friday. The entrance fee is 5 JD for adults and 1 JD for children.

The Royal Automobile Museum
This museum is a tribute to the late King Hussein's love for cars. It showcases a rare collection of Jordan's vehicles ranging from Hussein's cars and motorcycles to classic cars. The museum is located in King Hussein Park in Amman and is open from 10:00 AM to 7:00 PM from Tuesday to Sunday. The entrance fee is 3 JD for adults and 2 JD for children.

The Children's Museum

A great place for kids, this museum offers a variety of interactive and educational exhibits. It's located in Al Hussein Public Parks and is open from 9:00 AM to 7:00 PM from Friday to Wednesday, and from 1:00 PM to 7:00 PM on Thursday. The entrance fee is 3 JD per person.

The Museum of Popular Traditions
This museum is located in the Roman Theatre complex and showcases a collection of traditional Jordanian and Palestinian costumes, as well as mosaics from Madaba and Jerash. The museum is open from 8:00 AM to 7:00 PM in the summer and from 8:00 AM to 4:00 PM in the winter. The entrance fee is included in the Roman Theatre's admission ticket, which is 2 JD.

10.6 Museums in Jerash

Jerash Archaeological Museum
The Jerash Archaeological Museum, https://museums.visitjordan.com/en/Museum/32. was established in 1985 and houses a collection of artifacts from various eras that the region has passed through, starting from the Roman era. The exhibits include coins, glassware, and household items. The museum was initially established in 1923 inside one of the vaults of the courtyard of the

Artemis Temple, but it was moved to its current location in 1985. The museum is committed to preserving various historical artifacts from the Jerash Governorate, making it one of the oldest museums in Jordan.

10.7 Museums in Petra

Petra Museum
The Petra Museum is a must-visit for history and archaeology enthusiasts. It houses a marvelous collection of ancient artifacts related to Petra, with most of the exhibits being related to the Nabatean civilization. The museum contains 280 artifacts, dating back to different ages, providing a comprehensive insight into the rich history of the region. It is conveniently located next to the Visitor Center at the entrance to the Petra Archaeological Park.

This museum is a great place to see some of the most important artifacts and learn about the history and culture of the region.

Old Petra Museum

The Old Petra Museum is another archaeological museum in the city of Petra. It is uniquely located inside the natural rock within one of the Nabataean structures. This museum offers a unique opportunity to explore the history of Petra in a setting that is part of the city's historical fabric.

10.8 Theatres in Amman, Jordan

Darat al Funun
Darat al Funun is a home for the arts and artists from the Arab world. They organize exhibitions, talks, film screenings and also offer a PhD fellowship and an artist residency. The theatre is located in a beautiful setting and offers a variety of performances throughout the year. For more information about their schedule and ticket prices, you can visit their website at https://daratalfunun.org/.

Odeon Theater
The Odeon Theater is a popular venue for various cultural events in Amman. It hosts a variety of performances including plays, concerts, and film screenings. The Odeon Theater is known for its

unique architecture and its contribution to the cultural scene in Amman.

Rainbow Art House Theatre
Rainbow Art House Theatre is a small independent theatre that offers a variety of performances and events. It is a great place to experience local and international art and culture. The theatre is located in the heart of Amman and is a popular spot for both locals and tourists.

TAJ Cinemas
TAJ Cinemas is the largest cinema complex in Jordan. It is spread over 7000 m² and seats a total of 1700 people through its 16 theatre multiplex that includes 12 regular theatres. They offer a variety of movies from different genres. For more information about their schedule and ticket prices, you can visit their website (https://tajcinemas.com/)

Grand Cinemas
Grand Cinemas is a popular cinema chain in Jordan. They offer a variety of movies from different genres. They are known for their comfortable seating and high-quality screens. For more information about their schedule and ticket prices, you can visit their website (https://jo.grandcinemasme.com/)

Prime Cinemas
Prime Cinemas is another popular cinema chain in Jordan. They offer a variety of movies from different genres. They are known for their comfortable seating and high-quality screens. For more information about their schedule and ticket prices, you can visit their website (https://www.prime.jo/)

10.9 Nightlife in Amman, Jordan

Amman has a modest but lively nightlife scene centered in certain districts like Jebel Weibdeh, Jebel Amman, and Shmeisani. The busiest nights are Thursday, Friday, and Saturday when most places stay open late. Things tend to wind down early on Sundays through Wednesdays. Dress is generally casual at most venues. But avoid shorts or sleeveless tops, especially at upscale clubs.

Top Nightlife Spots

- **Rainbow Street** - This vibrant, walkable street in Jebel Amman comes alive at night with busy shisha lounges, pubs, artsy cafes and street food until late. Fun area to bar hop.
- **Sufra Restaurant** - Popular rainbow street spot for drinks and dancing. They host DJs and live music weekend nights. Gets crowded so come early.
- **Cantaloupe Gastro Pub** - Trendy but casual gastropub on Rainbow Street. Extensive drink menu includes Jordanian craft beers on tap. Livens up late.
- **Jadal Culture House** - Unique bookstore transform into a cozy bar at night located near the 1st Circle. Relaxed spot for conversation over local beers and wine.
- **Flip Flop Camp Bar** - Chilled open-air bar in Al-Weibdeh with cheap drinks and good shisha. No cover. Great for backpackers and young crowd.
- **Cafe De Paris** - Shmeisani piano bar with nightly live music. Classy French colonial style balcony setting. Cocktails and wine only.
- **Sekrab** - Sekrab is a popular spot for nightlife in Amman. It's known for its lively atmosphere and unique decor made from recycled materials. They offer a variety of drinks and often have live music or DJs playing.
- **Ghoroub Sunset Bar and Lounge** - Located at the top of the Landmark Amman Hotel, Ghoroub Sunset Bar and Lounge offers stunning views of the city. It's a great place to relax and enjoy a drink while watching the sunset.
- **Murphy's House of Rock** - Murphy's House of Rock is a popular bar that often features live rock music. It's a great place to let loose and enjoy the music.
- **Amigo Pub** - Amigo Pub is a cozy spot that offers a wide selection of drinks and often has live music. It's a great place to unwind after a day of sightseeing.

Getting Around at Night

- Taxis are plentiful and most reliable way to bar hop. Uber and Careem also operate. Agree on fare before riding.
- Bring small bills - drivers rarely have change for large notes. Most rides within Amman run 2-5 JDs.
- Travel in groups late at night and only take registered taxi or rideshare cars. Ask your hotel to arrange a pickup when ready.

Remember, the nightlife in Jordan can be quite different from what you might be used to. Many places, especially cafes, stay open late and offer a relaxed spot to people-watch with some herbal tea and shisha.

11   Day Trips and Excursions

11.1 One Day in Amman for First-Time Visitors

08:00 - Start at Rainbow Street
Start your day at Rainbow Street, located in the Jebel Amman district. This vibrant area is known for its restaurants, cafes, and funky decorations. Take a stroll and soak in the atmosphere.

09:00 - Breakfast at Nabteh O Fatteh
Stop for breakfast at Nabteh O Fatteh and try their delicious traditional meals.

10:00 - Visit the Grand Husseini Mosque
Take a 15-minute downhill walk to the Grand Husseini Mosque, one of the oldest mosques in Amman. Remember to dress appropriately (cover your shoulders and knees) if you plan to enter the mosque.

11:00 - Explore Souq Bukharia
Right across the street from the Grand Husseini Mosque is Souq Bukharia, the perfect place to shop for souvenirs in Amman.

12:00 - Visit the Roman Theatre
Next, head to the incredible Roman Theatre. Dating from the 2nd century, the Roman Theatre could seat about 6,000 people. The entrance costs 2 Jod per person, but it's free for Jordan Pass holders.

14:00 - Visit the Amman Citadel
After lunch, visit the Amman Citadel. The ruins here are from the Roman, Byzantine, and Umayyad periods. The citadel offers some of the best views over Amman. The entrance fee is 2 Jod, but it's free for Jordan Pass holders.

16:00 - Late Lunch at Hashem Restaurant
By the time you finish exploring the citadel, you'll be hungry. Stop at Amman's most famous restaurant - Hashem. This restaurant serves delicious traditional food at affordable prices.

18:00 - Visit The Duke's Diwan
Continue your Amman one-day itinerary with The Duke's Diwan, a traditional Jordanian home that gives you a glimpse into how the Jordanian people used to live.
19:00 - Dessert at Habibah Sweets
End the day with something sweet. Habibah Sweets sells the most delicious Kenafah. This dessert is made from pastry soaked in sugary syrup and layered with cheese.

20:00 - 23:00 - Free Time
Spend the rest of your evening exploring the city at your own pace. You could return to Rainbow Street for dinner, or perhaps find a cozy cafe to relax in.

Tips:
o   Dress appropriately as the majority of Jordanian people are Muslim. Dress conservatively and cover your shoulders and knees.
o   Stay hydrated as summer days can be extremely hot. Also, don't forget to apply sunscreen!
o   Bargaining is acceptable when shopping for souvenirs.
o   The locals are kind and welcoming. Don't hesitate to interact with them.

11.1.1 One Day in Amman map

Interactive link to the map: https://bit.ly/3P4ARCN

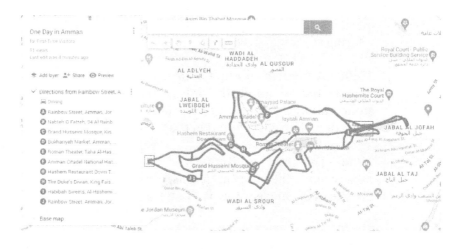

11.2 From Amman: Jerash, Ajloun Castle or Umm Qais Private Tour

Below is a detailed itinerary for the one-day tour titled "From Amman: Jerash, Ajloun Castle or Umm Qais Private Tour". Please note that the exact timing may vary depending on the traffic and other factors.

08:00 - Departure from Amman
Start your day by departing from your hotel in Amman. You will be picked up by a private vehicle that will take you to your first destination.

09:30 - Arrival at Jerash
Your first stop is the ancient city of Jerash, one of the most well-preserved Greco-Roman cities in the world. Here, you can explore the colonnaded streets, the temples of Artemis and Zeus, and the Oval Plaza. You will also see the Nymphaeum, a Roman public fountain that is considered one of the finest monuments in Jerash.

12:00 - Lunch
Enjoy a local lunch at a restaurant in Jerash. This is a great opportunity to try some traditional Jordanian dishes.

13:30 - Departure to Ajloun Castle
After lunch, you will head to Ajloun Castle, a 12th-century Muslim castle situated in northwestern Jordan. The castle was built by

145

one of Saladin's generals and is located on top of Mount 'Auf, offering stunning views of the Jordan Valley.

15:00 - Arrival at Ajloun Castle
Explore the Ajloun Castle with its beautiful arches and intricate stone carvings. The castle also houses a small museum with a collection of artifacts found in the region.

17:00 - Departure to Umm Qais
Next, you will head to Umm Qais, a town in northern Jordan near the site of the ancient town of Gadara.

18:30 - Arrival at Umm Qais
At Umm Qais, you can explore the ruins of the ancient Roman city of Gadara, with its colonnaded street, a two-story basilica, and an impressive black basalt theatre.

20:00 - Dinner
End your day with a delicious dinner at a local restaurant in Umm Qais. After dinner, you will be transported back to your hotel in Amman.

23:00 - Arrival at Amman
Arrive back at your hotel in Amman and rest for the night.

11.2.1 From Amman: Jerash, Ajloun Castle or Umm Qais

map

Interactive link to the map: https://bit.ly/3EsHvOk

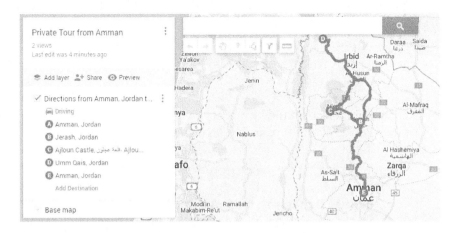

Private Tour from Amman

2 views
Last edit was 4 minutes ago

Add layer   Share   Preview

Directions from Amman, Jordan t...

Driving

A Amman, Jordan
B Jerash, Jordan
C Ajloun Castle, عجلون قلعة. Ajlou...
D Umm Qais, Jordan
E Amman, Jordan

Add Destination

Base map

Please note that the prices for the tour can start from **US$ 249 per person**. The tour includes transportation but does not include entrance fees to the sites or meals. The exact price may vary depending on the date and the number of people in the group. You can book the tour and find more information on the official website.

147

12 Amman: Petra, Wadi Rum, and Dead Sea 2-Day Tour

Below is a detailed itinerary for a two-day tour from Amman to Petra, Wadi Rum, and Dead Sea.

12.1 Day One: Amman to Petra

08:00 - Departure from Amman
Start your day early and get ready for an exciting adventure. You will be picked up from your hotel in Amman and begin the journey to Petra.

10:30 - Arrival at Petra
After a 2.5-hour drive, you will arrive at the ancient city of Petra, a UNESCO World Heritage Site and one of the New Seven Wonders of the World.

10:30 - 14:00 - Exploring Petra
Spend the next few hours exploring the rock-carved city of Petra. You will see the famous Al-Khazneh (The Treasury), the Royal Tombs, the Monastery, and many other fascinating sights. Don't forget to take plenty of photos!

14:00 - 15:00 - Lunch
Take a break and enjoy a local meal at one of the restaurants in Petra.

15:00 - 18:00 - Continue Exploring Petra
After lunch, continue exploring the hidden gems of Petra. Make sure to check out the Street of Facades, the Great Temple, and the Byzantine Church.

18:00 - Departure to Wadi Rum
At the end of the day, you will depart Petra and head towards Wadi Rum, also known as the Valley of the Moon.

20:00 - Arrival at Wadi Rum and Dinner

Upon arrival at Wadi Rum, you will check into a Bedouin camp where you will spend the night. Enjoy a traditional Bedouin dinner and experience the hospitality of the desert people.

21:00 - 23:00 - Stargazing

End your day by gazing at the stars in the clear desert sky. The lack of light pollution in Wadi Rum makes it an ideal place for stargazing.

Remember to wear comfortable shoes as there will be a lot of walking. Also, don't forget to bring a hat, sunscreen, and plenty of water to stay hydrated. Enjoy your trip!

12.1.1 Amman to Petra Map

Interactive link to the map: https://bit.ly/ammantopetra

12.2 Day 2: Wadi Rum and Dead Sea

08:00 - 10:00: Breakfast and Departure to Wadi Rum
Start your day with a hearty breakfast at your Bedouin camp. After breakfast, prepare for a journey to the stunning desert landscape of Wadi Rum.

10:00 - 12:00: Wadi Rum Exploration
Upon arrival at Wadi Rum, you will embark on a thrilling exploration of this desert wilderness. Known as the Valley of the Moon, Wadi Rum is famous for its red-pink sands, dramatic rock formations, and stunning panoramas. You might recognize the landscape from films like "Lawrence of Arabia" and "The Martian".

12:00 - 14:00: Lunch and Relaxation
After your desert adventure, you'll have a chance to relax and enjoy a delicious lunch. This is a great opportunity to try traditional Jordanian dishes.

14:00 - 16:00: Departure to Dead Sea
Post lunch, you will depart for the Dead Sea, the lowest point on earth. The drive itself is scenic and enjoyable.

16:00 - 19:00: Dead Sea Experience
Once you reach the Dead Sea, prepare for a unique experience. The high salt content of the sea allows you to float effortlessly on the surface. Don't forget to apply the mineral-rich mud on your skin for a natural spa experience.

19:00 - 21:00: Dinner and Relaxation
After your Dead Sea adventure, you'll have time to relax and enjoy a well-deserved dinner.

21:00 - 23:00: Return to Amman
As the day comes to an end, you will return to Amman. Reflect on the amazing experiences and memories you've made over the past two days as you journey back to the city.

For more details and booking, please visit the official tour page here.

Price: The starting price for this 2-day tour is US$ 249 per person. Please check the official tour page for the most accurate and up-to-date pricing information.

12.2.1 Day 2: Wadi Rum and Dead Sea Map

Interactive link to the map: https://bit.ly/wadirumdeadsea

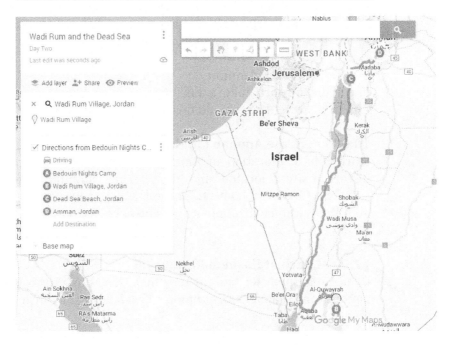

13 The Best 6 Day Jordan Itinerary for First Time Visitors

Below is a suggested itinerary for a 6-day trip to Jordan which includes Amman, Petra, Wadi Rum, and the Dead Sea.

13.1 Day One: Amman

08:00 - Arrival at Queen Alia International Airport
Start your journey by landing at Queen Alia International Airport. It's the main airport in Jordan and is located in Zizya, 30 kilometers south of the capital city, Amman.

09:00 - Travel to Amman
From the airport, take a taxi or a service like Uber to reach Amman. The journey should take around 45 minutes.

10:00 - Visit the Amman Citadel
Start your exploration of Amman at the Amman Citadel. This historical site is located on a hill, offering stunning views of the city. The Citadel is home to ancient ruins of Roman, Byzantine, and Umayyad civilizations. The entrance fee is 3 JD (around $4.25).

12:00 - Lunch at Hashem Restaurant
Head to Hashem Restaurant for lunch. This downtown eatery is famous for its falafel and hummus. It's a favorite among locals and tourists alike.

13:00 - Explore the Roman Theater
After lunch, visit the Roman Theater. This 2nd-century theater is a famous landmark in Amman. It was built during the reign of Antoninus Pius (138-161 CE). The theater is cut into the northern side of a hill, and it can seat 6000 people.

15:00 - Stroll in the Rainbow Street
Next, take a stroll down Rainbow Street. It's a vibrant area with plenty of shops, cafes, and art galleries.

17:00 - Visit the King Abdullah Mosque

Head to the King Abdullah Mosque. This blue-domed mosque is a beautiful sight to behold. Non-Muslim visitors are allowed inside outside of prayer times.

19:00 - Dinner at Sufra Restaurant
For dinner, go to Sufra Restaurant on Rainbow Street. This restaurant offers a variety of traditional Jordanian dishes.

21:00 - Return to your hotel
After a long day of sightseeing, return to your hotel and rest for the next day's adventures.

13.2 Day 2: Amman to Petra

08:00: Depart from Amman to Petra.
The journey will take approximately 3 hours, however 4 hours are allowed for any stops.

12:00: Arrive in Petra
Explore the ancient city. You can visit the famous Al-Khazneh (the Treasury), the Royal Tombs, the Monastery, and more. Don't forget to take plenty of photos!

13:00: Lunch
Have lunch at one of the local restaurants in Petra.

14:00 - 18:00 Continue exploring Petra.
You can also hire a local guide to learn more about the history and culture of this ancient city.

19:00: Have dinner at your hotel and rest for the night.

You can book a tour like the "Amman: Petra, Wadi Rum, and Dead Sea 2-Day Tour"(https://bit.ly/3LdV9c6) which covers Petra and other attractions in Jordan.

13.2.1 Map from Amman to Petra

Interactive link to the map

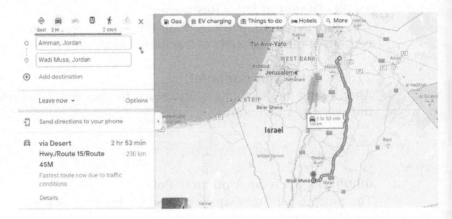

13.3 Day 3: Travel to Wadi Rum

08:00: Depart from Petra to Wadi Rum.
The journey is about 2 hours.

10:00: Arrive in Wadi Rum
Start exploring the desert. You can take a jeep tour, go on a camel ride, or even take a hot air balloon ride.

13:00: Have lunch at a local Bedouin camp.

14:00 - 18:00: Continue exploring Wadi Rum.
Don't miss the opportunity to see the stunning desert landscapes and rock formations.

19:00: Dinner and stayover in Wadi Rum

You can book a tour like the "Wadi Rum: Half-Day 5 Hour Jeep Tour with Overnight and Meals"(https://bit.ly/45UgDmJ) which covers Wadi Rum and includes meals and overnight stay.

13.3.1 Map from Petra to Wadi Rum Village

Note, the map states Petra as Wadi Rum.

Interactive link to the map

13.4 Day 4: Wadi Rum to the Dead Sea

08:00: Have breakfast at your hotel.

09:00: Depart for the Dead Sea
Allow 5 hours for this journey.

14:00: Arrival at the Dead Sea
Check in at your hotel for a two-night stay.

14:30: Have lunch at your hotel

15:30 – 18:00: Relax at the Dead Sea
Spend the afternoon relaxing at the Dead Sea. You can float in the mineral-rich waters, apply the therapeutic mud on your skin, or simply relax by the beach.

19:00: Dinner at your hotel and rest for the night

13.4.1 Map from Wadi Rum to the Dead Sea

<u>Interactive link to the map</u>

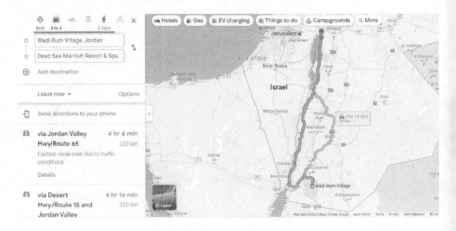

13.5 Day 5: Enjoying the Dead Sea

08:00: Breakfast
Enjoy a relaxing breakfast at your hotel or in a restaurant

09:00: Spend the morning visiting some of the attractions
You can visit the nearby attractions like the Baptism Site of Jesus
Christ or the ancient city of Jericho.

13:00: Lunch
Have lunch in a local restaurant.

14:00 - 18:00: Dead Sea
Relaxing at the Dead Sea.
Spend the afternoon relaxing at the Dead Sea.

19:00: Dinner
Have dinner at your hotel and rest for the night.

13.6 Day 6: Travel back to Amman

08:00: Breakfast
Have breakfast at your hotel and check out.

09:00: Depart from the Dead Sea to Amman.
The journey only takes about an hour.

11:00: Arrive in Amman
Spend the rest of the day relaxing.

Please note that the times are approximate and may vary depending on the traffic and other factors.

13.6.1 Map from the Dead Sea to Amman

Interactive link to the map

157

14   Conclusion

As we wrap up this comprehensive guide to the captivating country of Jordan, it's clear that this Middle Eastern gem is a must-visit destination for any avid traveler. From the ancient city of Petra, carved into rose-red stone cliffs, to the vast, otherworldly landscapes of Wadi Rum, Jordan is a country that effortlessly blends history, culture, and natural beauty.

The capital city of Amman is a bustling metropolis where modernity and tradition coexist, offering a vibrant mix of shopping, dining, and historical sites. The Roman ruins of Jerash and the Byzantine mosaics of Madaba provide fascinating glimpses into the country's rich history, while the therapeutic waters of the Dead Sea offer a unique and relaxing experience.

Jordanian cuisine, with its mouthwatering array of dishes like mansaf, falafel, and hummus, is sure to delight food lovers. The country's strong tradition of hospitality means visitors will feel warmly welcomed, whether they're exploring the bustling souks or enjoying a cup of traditional Bedouin tea.

Despite its many attractions, Jordan remains a safe and easy country to travel in, with modern infrastructure and a wide range of accommodations to suit all budgets. English is widely spoken, particularly in the tourism sector, making it easy for travelers to navigate their way around.

However, the true magic of Jordan lies in the unexpected moments that you'll encounter along the way - a stunning sunset over the desert, a warm welcome from a local, or the awe-inspiring sight of Petra emerging from the shadows at dawn.
In conclusion, Jordan is a country that captivates and surprises, leaving a lasting impression on all who visit. Whether you're a history buff, a nature lover, a foodie, or simply an intrepid traveler looking for your next adventure, Jordan offers an unforgettable journey that will touch your heart and ignite your sense of wonder.

So pack your bags, open your mind, and prepare to fall in love with Jordan - a land of ancient history, diverse cultures, and unparalleled natural beauty. Your Jordanian adventure awaits!

Made in the USA
Las Vegas, NV
14 December 2023

82776164R00089